T0319006

SELECTIONS FROM PLAUTUS

SELECTIONS
from PLAUTUS

With INTRODUCTION
and NOTES by

K. M. WESTAWAY, D. LIT. (Lond.)

Late Marion Kennedy Student, Newnham College
Staff-Lecturer in Classics, Royal Holloway College

CAMBRIDGE
AT THE UNIVERSITY PRESS
MCMXXIV

CAMBRIDGE UNIVERSITY PRESS
Cambridge, New York, Melbourne, Madrid, Cape Town,
Singapore, São Paulo, Delhi, Mexico City

Cambridge University Press
The Edinburgh Building, Cambridge CB2 8RU, UK

Published in the United States of America by Cambridge University Press, New York

www.cambridge.org
Information on this title: www.cambridge.org/9781107620056

First published 1924
First paperback edition 2013

A catalogue record for this publication is available from the British Library

ISBN 978-1-107-62005-6 Paperback

PREFACE

THIS little book is intended for readers in schools and colleges who are preparing for those examinations in which the Latin unseen translation demands a certain knowledge of Plautus. Hitherto this knowledge has generally been acquired by the complete reading of a single play, probably the *Captiui* or the *Trinummus*. Excellent as both these plays are from the dramatic standpoint, neither of them shows Plautus at his liveliest and best, and neither of them is properly typical of Plautus as a comic writer. Classical teachers have long felt the need of a series of short readings that shall be most representative of Plautus and most attractive to the average reader.

Plautus is not nearly so well known among our students of Latin as he deserves. The result has been a lamentable gap in the survey which the pupil gradually makes, through his translation lessons, of Latin literature. Plautus is the earliest extant Latin writer, and therefore an invaluable source of our knowledge of an age which, apart from him, has left us no literary expression of itself. He is, moreover, master of a form of literature from which we gain a peculiarly intimate acquaintance with the ordinary people of his day. Lastly, Plautus is one of the greatest linguistic monuments which we possess in Latin. His readiness of expression and his fertility of imagination are revealed in every page of every play. Hardly anywhere else do we find such a satisfying insight into the *sermo cotidianus* of the Romans. It is not surprising that, without an acquaintance with Plautus, the pupil can gain but a very inadequate notion of Roman ways of thought and expression, and it is hoped that these specimens of Plautine frolic will give him a new and more entertaining idea of what Latin may become to those who have the opportunity to read, and the mind to appreciate, such a treasury of good things. These extracts are offered, not as a substitute for whole plays, but as an introduction and inducement to further reading in the works of one of Rome's most lively and amusing authors.

No attempt is here made at a critical text; in almost every detail the Oxford text of Professor Lindsay has been followed. The notes are intended for readers who are more than beginners in Latin—who are, in fact, already acquainted with Caesar, Cicero, and Vergil, but who are here introduced to Plautus for the first time. It is particularly recommended that they should be made to read the introduction as well as the text and notes: this is a sign of grace which does not always reveal itself even in the mature reader. A short appendix on metre is given. For the details of Plautine prosody and metre (a subject fascinating in itself, but vast and intricate and beyond the needs of the beginner in Plautus), the more enterprising student is referred to the excellent excursus in Lindsay's introduction to the *Captiui* (Methuen, 1900).

K. M. WESTAWAY.

February 1924.

CONTENTS

INTRODUCTION

PLAUTUS is the most ancient of extant Latin writers. It is not surprising that at this distance of time we know little of his life and of the conditions under which he worked, but from Aulus Gellius (a Roman critic of the second century A.D.) we learn the following facts about him.

He was born about 254 B.C., of poor parents, at Sarsina in Umbria (Central Italy), and came to Rome and worked there as a stage-carpenter, or possibly as an actor. In this way he made some money, but he lost it through speculations in foreign trade. He then hired himself to a miller, and in his leisure time wrote plays and sold them. He died in 184 B.C.

His life was thus one of continual hard work and poverty. His hardships were probably all the greater since his career included the whole period of the second Punic war, which devastated Italy and brought warfare practically to the gates of Rome. It was only towards the end of this war that comedies came to be written and acted at Rome at all. Perhaps the relaxation from the prolonged strain of fighting was responsible for the people's newly-discovered aptitude for this form of amusement. Not long before Plautus, Livius Andronicus and Naevius wrote comedies, but their works have not come down to us. Additional value is thus attached to Plautus since he is such a solitary representative of his age and type.

In later ages, a hundred and thirty plays passed under Plautus' name, but Varro (a critic of the first century B.C.) recognised as genuine only twenty-one. Of these, twenty have survived to the present day, and the remaining play, the *Vidularia*, exists for us in inconsiderable fragments. In any case, he seems to have been a most prolific writer.

Plautus' plays are, in the main, translations or adaptations from the [Greek] New Comedy, which was written at Athens by dramatists such as Menander and Philemon, during the years which followed the death of Alexander the Great. As the works of all these Greek writers have perished, except for a few fragments, it is impossible to estimate the literalness of Plautus' versions. In every case he appears to retain the Greek scene of his originals, the Greek names of the characters, and many Greek customs. His plays are thus what are technically called *fabulae palliatae* (so-called from the *pallium*, or Greek cloak), as distinct from the *fabulae togatae*, which were the national Roman comedies (deriving their name from the Roman *toga*). There was, in Plautus' day, a strict state-censorship of plays, and this prevented the representation on the stage of politicians and public personalities, or even of Roman social life in any marked degree. Naevius wrote *fabulae togatae*, which, from their very nature, offended against these regulations, and he was imprisoned for his pains. Nevertheless, although Plautus chose the more discreet course of producing *fabulae palliatae*, much of the manner and spirit of his plays is thoroughly Roman, and a perusal of his works gives us an insight into the habits and thoughts of the Rome of his day. Thus, in the extracts in this little book, the accounts of the military exploits of *Amphitruo* and of the *Miles Gloriosus* are highly suggestive of the character of the warfare employed by Rome in that age, and the passage from the *Captiui* contains a portrait of a parasite who was quite as characteristic of Roman social life as of Greek. In stray details, too, the reader will notice many Roman touches (for example, the puns on Italian place-names in the passage from the *Captiui*), which cannot be derived from a Greek author, but must be original to Plautus. Always in reading these plays one may notice the parallel contributions of Greek and Roman thought.

It is not only for his value as practically the sole literary expression of an early age, that we read Plautus. We must needs take a delight in his wonderful gift of fun and frolic. Although a translator, he is the most spontaneous of writers, and although he may not have credit for the varied devices of his plots (for these he derived directly from his originals), yet he presents his scenes with a vitality which must be all his own. An analysis of so exuberant a style seems artificial, if not impossible. The reader must observe it for himself, in order to arrive at a personal—which is the only real —appreciation of it. The style is thoroughly colloquial and idiomatic, and is marked by many features characteristic of the native Latin language, e.g. alliteration, assonance, and asyndeton. Plautus frequently enlivens his style by puns, by a wealth of metaphor, and by a most exuberant vocabulary of terms of abuse and endearment. Certainly his language is unique in Latin literature, and yet it is so natural and unforced, that we cannot believe that it was anything but typical of the gifted and versatile people to whom he belonged.

Dramatic representations took place at Rome only on certain occasions, namely, at the public festivals—the *Ludi Megalenses* (April 4–9), *Ludi Apollinares* (July 6), *Ludi Romani* (September 4–12), and *Ludi Plebeii* (November 16–18). Now and again they were given on private occasions, for example at the funeral of a distinguished Roman.

There was no stone theatre at Rome until the time of Pompey, who was responsible for the erection of one in 55 B.C. In Plautus' day plays were acted in temporary wooden theatres, which had no roof and only very simple scenery. The spectators in all probability had to stand to watch the performances. The stage was very wide, but not deep. Generally it represented a street in a Greek town, with two houses, separated by a narrow passage to form the background. The action of each play has therefore to take place in the street. Thus in our first extract (from the *Amphitruo*) Mercury stands outside Amphitruo's house in order to bar the entrance to the slave Sosia; and in our second (from the *Mostellaria*) Tranio talks to his master outside his own house, which has been shut up in accordance with the requirements of the plot. On the Roman stage, the entrance on the left of the spectators was always assumed to lead to the harbour, and that on the right to the market-place.

The plays were acted only by men. The actors who impersonated women wore masks. It is probable, though not certain, that those who impersonated men wore, not masks, but wigs, and had their faces painted.

The constituent parts of a Roman comedy, apart from the prologue which usually introduces the story, are the *diuerbium*, i.e. the dialogue and colloquial part, e.g. the whole of our extract from the *Miles Gloriosus*; and the *canticum* or lyrical monologue, accompanied by the flute, e.g. the lament of Palaestra in our extract from the *Rudens*. The plays of Plautus contain far more of the latter element than do those of Terence. The flute-player (*tibicen*) contributed much to a Roman dramatic performance, for, besides accompanying the *cantica*, he filled the short intervals in the play during which the stage was empty.

SELECTIONS FROM PLAUTUS

I

A Strange Dilemma
(*Amphitruo*, ll. 336–462, 551–632)

[This play is founded on an old Greek legend. While
Amphitruo was absent from Thebes on a campaign against
the Teleboans, Juppiter disguised himself as Amphitruo
and lived at Thebes as if he were the general himself.
Mercury, to bear him company, assumed the form of
Amphitruo's slave Sosia, and performed the menial
offices appropriate to his novel station. Amphitruo, on
his return from the war, sent Sosia in advance to announce
his arrival to his wife Alcmena. When Sosia came to the
entrance of the house, he found to his surprise another
Sosia, in fact Mercury, walking up and down, and re-
counting to himself with relish the number of people he
had injured and slain by his pugnacious proclivities. When
Sosia persisted in his errand, his way was barred by his
mysterious double. In the first of the scenes given here,
Mercury accosts the dismayed Sosia, and tries to per-
suade him that he is not really Sosia, but another man,
and in the second scene Sosia, half convinced, endeavours
to explain the situation to his master.]

SCENE I

SOSIA   MERCURIUS

So. Non edepol nunc ubi terrarum sim scio, si quis
                                               roget,
neque miser me commouere possum prae formidine.
ilicet: mandata eri perierunt una et Sosia.
uerum certumst confidenter hominem contra conloqui,
qui possim uideri huic fortis, a me ut apstineat manum.
ME. quo ambulas tu qui Volcanum in cornu conclusum
                                               geris?

So. quid id exquiris tu qui pugnis os exossas hominibus?

Me. seruo'sne an liber?   So. utquomque animo con-
                                        libitum est meo.

Me. aïn uero?   So. aio enim uero.   Me. uerbero.
                                        So. mentire nunc.

10 Me. at iam faciam ut uerum dicas dicere.   So. quid
                                        eo est opus?

Me. possum scire quo profectus, quoius sis aut quid
                                        ueneris?

So. huc eo. eri sum seruos. numquid nunc es certior?

Me. ego tibi istam hodie, sceleste, comprimam linguam.
                                        So. hau potes:

bene pudiceque adseruatur.   Me. pergin argutarier?

15 quid apud hasce aedis negoti est tibi?   So. immo, quid
                                        tibi est?

Me. rex Creo uigiles nocturnos singulos semper locat.

So. bene facit: quia nos eramus peregri, tutatust domi;

at nunc abi sane, aduenisse familiaris dicito.

Me. nescio quam tu familiaris sis: nisi actutum hinc abis,

20 familiaris, accipiere faxo hau familiariter.

So. hic, inquam, habito ego atque horunc seruos sum.
                                        Me. at scin quo modo?

faciam ego hodie te superbum, nisi hinc abis.   So. quo-
                                        nam modo?

Me. auferere, non abibis, si ego fustem sumpsero.

So. quin me esse huiius familiai familiarem praedico.

25 Me. uide sis quam mox uapulare uis, nisi actutum hinc
                                        abis.

So. tun domo prohibere peregre me aduenientem pos-
                                        tulas?

Me. haecine tua domust?   So. ita inquam.   Me. quis
                                        erus est igitur tibi?

So. Amphitruo, qui nunc praefectust Thebanis legio-
                                        nibus,

quicum nupta est Alcumena.   Me. quid ais? quid
                                        nomen tibi est?

30 So. Sosiam uocant Thebani, Dauo prognatum patre.
ME. ne tu istic hodie malo tuo compositis mendaciis
aduenisti, audaciai columen, consutis dolis.
So. immo equidem tunicis consutis huc aduenio, non
dolis.
ME. at mentiris etiam: certo pedibus, non tunicis uenis.
35 So. ita profecto. ME. nunc profecto uapula ob men-
dacium.
So. non edepol uolo profecto. ME. at pol profecto
ingratiis.
hoc quidem 'profecto' certum est, non est arbitrarium.
So. tuam fidem obsecro. ME. tun te audes Sosiam
esse dicere,
qui ego sum? So. perii. ME. parum etiam, praeut
futurum est, praedicas.
40 quoius nunc es? So. tuo', nam pugnis usu fecisti
tuom.
pro fidem, Thebani ciues! ME. etiam clamas, carnufex?
loquere, quid uenisti? So. ut esset quem tu pugnis
caederes.
ME. quoius es? So. Amphitruonis, inquam, Sosia.
ME. ergo istoc magis,
quia uaniloquo's, uapulabis: ego sum, non tu, Sosia.
45 So. ita di faciant, ut tu potius sis atque ego te ut
uerberem.
ME. etiam muttis? So. iam tacebo. ME. quis tibi
erust? So. quem tu uoles.
ME. quid igitur? qui nunc uocare? So. nemo nisi
quem iusseris.
ME. Amphitruonis te esse aiebas Sosiam. So. peccaueram,
nam Amphitruonis socium ne me esse uolui dicere.
50 ME. scibam equidem nullum esse nobis nisi me seruom
Sosiam.
fugit te ratio. So. utinam istuc pugni fecissent tui.

ME. ego sum Sosia ille quem tu dudum esse aiebas
                                                    mihi.
So. obsecro ut per pacem liceat te adloqui, ut ne
                                                    uapulem.
ME. immo indutiae parumper fiant, si quid uis loqui.
55 So. non loquar nisi pace facta, quando pugnis plus
                                                    uales.
ME. dicito quid uis, non nocebo.   So. tuae fide credo?
                                                    ME. meae.
So. quid si falles?   ME. tum Mercurius Sosiae iratus
                                                    siet.
So. animum aduorte.   nunc licet mi libere quiduis
                                                    loqui.
Amphitruonis ego sum seruos Sosia.   ME. etiam denuo?
60 So. pacem feci, foedus feci. uera dico.   ME. uapula.
So. ut lubet quid tibi lubet fac, quoniam pugnis plus
                                                    uales;
uerum, utut es facturus, hoc quidem hercle hau reticebo
                                                    tamen.
ME. tu me uiuos hodie nunquam facies quin sim Sosia.
So. certe edepol tu me alienabis nunquam quin noster
                                                    siem;
65 nec praesente nobis alius quisquamst seruos Sosia.
qui cum Amphitruone hinc una iueram in exercitum.
ME. hic homo sanus non est.   So. quod mihi praedicas
                                                    uitium, id tibi est.
quid, malum, non sum ego seruos Amphitruonis Sosia?
nonne hac noctu nostra nauis huc ex portu Persico
70 uenit, quae me aduexit? non me huc erus misit meus?
nonne ego nunc sto ante aedis nostras? non mi est
                                                    lanterna in manu?
non loquor, non uigilo? nonne hic homo modo me
                                                    pugnis contudit?
fecit hercle, nam etiam mi misero nunc malae dolent.
quid igitur ego dubito, aut qur non intro eo in nostram
                                                    domum?

75 ME. quid, domum uostram?   So. ita enim uero.

     ME. quin quae dixisti modo

omnia ementitu's: equidem Sosia Amphitruoni sum.

nam noctu hac soluta est nauis nostra e portu Persico,

et ubi Pterela rex regnauit oppidum expugnauimus,

et legiones Teleboarum ui pugnando cepimus,

80 et ipsus Amphitruo optruncauit regem Pterelam in

                        proelio.

So. egomet mihi non credo, quom illaec autumare

                     illum audio;

hic quidem certe quae illic sunt res gestae memorat

                     memoriter.

sed quid ais? quid Amphitruoni a Telebois est datum?

ME. Pterela rex qui potitare solitus est patera aurea.

85 So. elocutus est. ubi patera nunc est? ME. est in

                     cistula;

Amphitruonis opsignata signo est. So. signi dic quid

                     est?

ME. cum quadrigis Sol exoriens. quid me captas,

                     carnufex?

So. argumentis uicit, aliud nomen quaerundum est mihi.

nescio unde haec hic spectauit. iam ego hunc decipiam

                     probe;

90 nam quod egomet solus feci, nec quisquam alius adfuit,

in tabernaclo, id quidem hodie nunquam poterit dicere.

si tu Sosia es, legiones quom pugnabant maxume,

quid in tabernaclo fecisti? uictus sum si dixeris.

ME. cadus erat uini, inde impleui hirneam. So. in-

                     gressust uiam.

95 ME. eam ego, ut matre fuerat natum, uini eduxi meri.

So. factumst illud, ut ego illic uini hirneam ebiberim

                     meri.

mira sunt nisi latuit intus illic in illac hirnea.

ME. quid nunc? uincon argumentis te non esse Sosiam?

So. tu negas med esse? ME. quid ego ni negem, qui

                     egomet siem?

100 So. per Iouem iuro med esse neque me falsum dicere.

    Me. at ego per Mercurium iuro tibi Iouem non credere;

    nam iniurato scio plus credet mihi quam iurato tibi.

    So. quis ego sum saltem, si non sum Sosia? te interrogo.

    Me. ubi ego Sosia nolim esse, tu esto sane Sosia;

105 nunc, quando ego sum, uapulabis, ni hinc abis, ignobilis.

    So. certe edepol, quom illum contemplo et formam
                                        cognosco meam,

    quem ad modum ego sum (saepe in speculum inspexi),
                                        nimi' similest mei;

    itidem habet petasum ac uestitum; tam consimilest
                                        atque ego;

    sura, pes, statura, tonsus, oculi, nasum uel labra,

110 malae, mentum, barba, collus: totus. quid uerbis opust?

    si tergum cicatricosum, nihil hoc similist similius.

    sed quom cogito, equidem certo idem sum qui semper fui.

    noui erum, noui aedis nostras; sane sapio et sentio.

    non ego illi optempero quod loquitur. pultabo fores.

115 Me. quo agis te? So. domum. Me. quadrigas si
                                    nunc inscendas Iouis

    atque hinc fugias, ita uix poteris ecfugere infortunium.

    So. nonne erae meae enuntiare quod erus meu' iussit licet?

    Me. tuae si quid uis nuntiare: hanc nostram adire non
                                        sinam.

    nam si me inritassis, hodie lumbifragium hinc auferes.

120 So. abeo potius. di inmortales, opsecro uostram fidem,

    ubi ego perii? ubi immutatus sum? ubi ego formam
                                        perdidi?

    an egomet me illic reliqui, si forte oblitus fui?

    nam hicquidem omnem imaginem meam, quae antehac
                                       fuerat, possidet.

    uiuo fit quod nunquam quisquam mortuo faciet mihi.

125 ibo ad portum atque haec uti sunt facta ero dicam meo;

    nisi etiam is quoque me ignorabit; quod ille faxit Iup-
                                        piter,

    ut ego hodie raso capite caluos capiam pilleum.

SCENE II

AMPHITRUO   SOSIA

AM. Age i tu secundum.   So. sequor, supsequor te.
AM. scelestissumum te arbitror.   So. nam quamobrem?
AM. quia id quod neque est neque fuit neque futurum
                                                    est
mihi praedicas.   So. eccere iam tuatim
5 facis, ut tuis nulla apud te fides sit.
   AM. quid est? quo modo? iam quidem hercle ego tibi
                                                    istam
scelestam, scelus, linguam apscidam.   So. tuos sum,
proinde ut commodumst et lubet quidque facias;
tamen quin loquar haec uti facta sunt hic,
10 nunquam ullo modo me potes deterrere.
   AM. scelestissume, audes mihi praedicare id,
domi te esse nunc qui hic ades?   So. uera dico.
   AM. malum quod tibi di dabunt, atque ego hodie
dabo.   So. istuc tibist in manu, nam tuos sum.
15 AM. tun me, uerbero, audes erum ludificari?
tune id dicere audes, quod nemo unquam homo
                                                    antehac
uidit, nec potest fieri, tempore uno
homo idem duobus locis ut simul sit?
   So. profecto ut loquor res ita est.   AM. Iuppiter te
20 perdat.   So. quid mali sum, ere, tua ex re promeritus?
   AM. rogasne, inprobe, etiam qui ludos facis me?
   So. merito maledicas mihi, si id ita factum est.
uerum hau mentior, resque uti facta dico.
         AM. homo hic ebrius est, ut opinor.
25   So. utinam ita essem.   AM. optas quae facta.
       So. egone?   AM. tu istic. ubi bibisti?
       So. nusquam equidem bibi.   AM. quid hoc sit
hominis?   So. equidem deciens dixi:
       domi ego sum, inquam, ecquid audis?

30　et apud te adsum Sosia idem.
　　satin hoc plane, satin diserte,
　　　　ere, nunc uideor
　　　　tibi locutus esse? Aм. uah,
　　apage te a me. So. quid est negoti?
35　Aм. pestis te tenet. So. nam qur istuc
　　dicis? equidem ualeo et saluos
　　sum recte, Amphitruo. Aм. at te ego faciam
　　　hodie proinde ac meritus es,
　　ut minu' ualeas et miser sis,
40　saluo' domum si rediero: iam
　　sequere sis, erum qui ludificas
　　　dictis delirantibus,
　qui quoniam eru' quod imperauit neglexisti persequi,
　nunc uenis etiam ultro inrisum dominum: quae neque
　　　　　　　　　　　　　　　　　　　　　fieri
45 possunt neque fando umquam accepit quisquam pro-
　　　　　　　　　　　　　　　　　　fers, carnufex;
　quoius ego hodie in tergum istaec faxo expetant men-
　　　　　　　　　　　　　　　　　　　　　dacia.
　So. Amphitruo, miserruma istaec miseria est seruo bono,
　apud erum qui uera loquitur, si id ui uerum uincitur.
　Aм. quo id, malum, pacto potest nam (mecum argu-
　　　　　　　　　　　　　　　　　　mentis puta)
50 fieri, nunc uti tu et hic sis et domi? id dici uolo.
　So. sum profecto et hic et illic. hoc quoiuis mirari licet.
　neque tibi istuc mirum mirum magi' uidetur quam
　　　　　　　　　　　　　　　　　　　　　mihi.
　Aм. quo modo? So. nihilo, inquam, mirum magi' tibi
　　　　　　　　　　　　　　　　　istuc quam mihi;
　neque, ita me di ament, credebam primo mihimet
　　　　　　　　　　　　　　　　　　　Sosiae,
55 donec Sosia illic egomet fecit sibi uti crederem.
　ordine omne, uti quidque actum est, dum apud hostis
　　　　　　　　　　　　　　　　　　sedimus,
　edissertauit. tum formam una apstulit cum nomine.

neque lact' lactis magis est simile quam ille ego similest
            mei.
nam ut dudum ante lucem a portu me praemisisti
            domum—
60 Am. quid igitur? So. priu' multo ante aedis stabam
          quam illo adueneram.
Am. quas, malum, nugas? satin tu sanus es? So. sic
          sum ut uides.
Am. huic homini nescioquid est mali mala obiectum
          manu,
postquam a me abiit. So. fateor, nam sum optusus
          pugnis pessume.
Am. quis te uerberauit? So. egomet memet, qui nunc
          sum domi.
65 Am. caue quicquam, nisi quod rogabo te, mihi respon-
          deris.
omnium primum iste qui sit Sosia, hoc dici uolo.
So. tuos est seruos. Am. mihi quidem uno te plus
         etiam est quam uolo,
neque postquam sum natus habui nisi te seruom Sosiam.
So. at ego nunc, Amphitruo, dico: Sosiam seruom
          tuom
70 praeter me alterum, inquam, adueniens faciam ut
         offendas domi,
Dauo prognatum patre eodem quo ego sum, forma,
         aetate item
qua ego sum. quid opust uerbis? geminus Sosia hic
         factust tibi.
Am. nimia memoras mira. sed uidistin uxorem meam?
So. quin intro ire in aedis nunquam licitum est. Am.
         quis te prohibuit?
75 So. Sosia ille quem iam dudum dico, is qui me contudit.
Am. quis istic Sosia est? So. ego, inquam. quotiens
         dicendum est tibi?
Am. sed quid ais? num obdormiuisti dudum? So. nus-
         quam gentium.

AM. ibi forte istum si uidisses quendam in somnis
                                        Sosiam.
So. non soleo ego somniculose eri imperia persequi.
80 uigilans uidi, uigilans nunc ut uideo, uigilans fabulor,
uigilantem ille me iam dudum uigilans pugnis contudit.
AM. quis homo?   So. Sosia, inquam ego ille. quaeso,
                                        nonne intellegis?
AM. qui, malum, intellegere quisquam potis est? ita
                                        nugas blatis.
So. uerum actutum nosces, quom illum nosces seruom
                                        Sosiam.
85 AM. sequere hac igitur me, nam mi istuc primum ex-
                                        quisito est opus.
sed uide ex naui ecferantur quae imperaui iam omnia.
So. et memor sum et diligens, ut quae imperes com-
                                        pareant;
non ego cum uino simitu ebibi imperium tuom.
AM. utinam di faxint infecta dicta re eueniant tua.

II

The Haunted House
(*Mostellaria*, 431–531)

[Philolaches, a young citizen of Athens, was one day
engaged at home in revels with a merry company of
friends, when the slave Tranio announced the unexpected
return from abroad of Theopropides, the young man's
father, of whose prolonged absence they had all taken
conspicuous advantage. In order to save his master in this
difficult situation, the ingenious slave directed the party to
close all the doors and windows of the house, thus making
it appear uninhabited, and to remain quiet within, while
he received the old man outside, and scared him summarily
and permanently off the premises by telling him that
his son had left the house because it was haunted. The
execution of this little plot is related in the following scene.]

THEOPROPIDES TRANIO

TH. Habeo, Neptune, gratiam magnam tibi,
quod med amisisti a te uix uiuom domum.
uerum si posthac me pedem latum modo
scies imposisse in undam, hau caussast ilico
5 quod nunc uoluisti facere quin facias mihi.
apage, apage te a me nunciam post hunc diem!
quod crediturus tibi fui omne credidi.
TR. edepol, Neptune, peccauisti largiter
qui occasionem hanc amisisti tam bonam.
10 TH. triennio post Aegypto aduenio domum;
credo exspectatus ueniam familiaribus.
TR. nimio edepol ille potuit exspectatior
uenire qui te nuntiaret mortuom.
TH. sed quid hoc? occlusa ianua est interdius.
15 pultabo. heus, ecquis istist? aperitin fores?
TR. quis homo est qui nostras aedis accessit prope?
TH. meu' seruos hicquidem est Tranio. TR. o Theopropides,
ere, salue, saluom te aduenisse gaudeo.
usquin ualuisti? TH. usque, ut uides. TR. factum
optume.
20 TH. quid uos? insanin estis? TR. quidum? TH. sic,
quia
foris ambulatis, natus nemo in aedibus
seruat neque qui recludat neque respondeat.
pultando paene confregi hasce ambas fores.
TR. eho an tu tetigisti has aedis? TH. qur non tangerem?
25 quin pultando, inquam, paene confregi fores.
TR. tetigistin? TH. tetigi, inquam, et pultaui. TR.
uah! TH. quid est?
TR. male hercle factum. TH. quid est negoti? TR.
non potest
dici quam indignum facinus fecisti et malum.

Th. quid iam? Tr. fuge, obsecro, atque abscede ab
aedibus.
30 fuge huc, fuge ad me propius. tetigistin fores?
Th. quomodo pultare potui, si non tangerem?
Tr. occidisti hercle— Th. quem mortalem? Tr. omnis
tuos.
Th. di te deaeque omnes faxint cum istoc omine—
Tr. metuo te atque istos expiare ut possies.
35 Th. quam ob rem? aut quam subito rem mihi adportas
nouam?
Tr. et heus, iube illos illinc ambo apscedere.
Th. apscedite. Tr. aedis ne attigatis. tangite
uos quoque terram. Th. opsecro hercle, quin eloquere
rem.
Tr. quia septem menses sunt quom in hasce aedis
pedem
40 nemo intro tetulit, semel ut emigrauimus.
Th. eloquere, quid ita? Tr. circumspicedum, num-
quis est
sermonem nostrum qui aucupet? Th. tutum probest.
Tr. circumspice etiam. Th. nemo est. loquere nunciam.
Tr. capitale scelu' factumst. Th. quid est? non in-
tellego.
45 Tr. scelus, inquam, factum est iam diu, antiquom et
uetus.
Th. antiquom? Tr. id adeo nos nunc factum in-
uenimus.
Th. quid istuc est sceleste? aut quis id fecit? cedo.
Tr. hospes necauit hospitem captum manu;
iste, ut ego opinor, qui has tibi aedis uendidit.
50 Th. necauit? Tr. aurumque ei ademit hospiti
eumque hic defodit hospitem ibidem in aedibus.
Th. quapropter id uos factum suspicamini?
Tr. ego dicam, ausculta. ut foris cenauerat
tuo' gnatus, postquam rediit a cena domum,

55 abimus omnes cubitum; condormiuimus:
   lucernam forte oblitus fueram exstinguere;
   atque ille exclamat derepente maxumum.
   TH. quis homo? an gnatus meus?   TR. st! tace, aus-
                                        culta modo.
   ait uenisse illum in somnis ad se mortuom.
60 TH. nempe ergo in somnis?   TR. ita. sed ausculta
                                        modo.
   ait illum hoc pacto sibi dixisse mortuom—
   TH. in somnis?   TR. mirum quin uigilanti diceret,
   qui abhinc sexaginta annis occisus foret.
   TH. taceo.   TR. sed ecce quae illi in somnis mortuos—
65 'ego transmarinus hospes sum Diapontius.
   hic habito, haec mihi dedita est habitatio.
   nam me Accheruntem recipere Orcus noluit,
   quia praemature uita careo. per fidem
   deceptus sum: hospes me hic necauit isque me
70 defodit insepultum clam in hisce aedibus,
   scelestus, auri caussa. nunc tu hinc emigra.
   scelestae sunt aedes, inpia est habitatio.'
   quae hic monstra fiunt anno uix possum eloqui.
   TH. st, st!
   TR. quid, opsecro hercle, factum est?   TH. concrepuit
                                                foris.
75 TR. hicin percussit!   TH. guttam haud habeo san-
                                                guinis,
   uiuom me accersunt Accheruntem mortui.
   TR. perii! illisce hodie hanc conturbabunt fabulam.
   nimi' quam formido ne manufesto hic me opprimat.
   TH. quid tute tecum loquere?   TR. apscede ab ianua.
80 fuge, obsecro hercle.   TH. quo fugiam? etiam tu fuge.
   TR. nihil ego formido, pax mihi est cum mortuis.
   INTUS. heus, Tranio!   TR. non me appellabis, si sapis.
   nihil ego commerui neque istas percussi fores.
   INTUS. quaeso— TR.* caue uerbum faxis.   TH. dic
                                        quid segreges

85 sermonem. TR. apage hinc te.   TH. quae res te*
                                              agitat, Tranio?
   quicum istaec loquere? TR. an quaeso tu appellaueras?
   ita me di amabunt, mortuom illum credidi
   expostulare quia percussisses fores.
   sed tu, etiamne astas nec quae dico optemperas?
90 TH. quid faciam? TR. caue respexis, fuge, operi caput.
   TH. qur non fugis tu? TR. pax mihi est cum mortuis.
   TH. scio. quid modo igitur? qur tanto opere extim-
                                              ueras?
   TR. nil me curassis, inquam, ego mihi prouidero:
   tu, ut occepisti, tantum quantum quis fuge
95 atque Herculem inuoca.   TH. Hercules, ted inuoco.—
   TR. et ego—tibi hodie ut det, senex, magnum malum.
   pro di immortales, opsecro uostram fidem!
   quid ego hodie negoti confeci mali.

III

The Braggart Captain
(*Miles Gloriosus*, ll. 1–57)

[Pyrgopolinices was a vain boastful soldier whose
prowess was related in words more often than it was
proved by deeds. In the following conversation between
him and his obsequious friend the parasite Artotrogus,
we learn of many feats of which the glory is, quite trans-
parently, too good to be true.]

PYRGOPOLINICES   ARTOTROGUS

PY. Curate ut splendor meo sit clupeo clarior
quam solis radii esse olim quom sudumst solent,
et, ubi usus ueniat, contra conserta manu
praestringat oculorum aciem in acie hostibus.

* Leo

5 nam ego hanc machaeram mihi consolari uolo,
   ne lamentetur neue animum despondeat,
   quia se iam pridem feriatam gestitem,
   quae misera gestit fartem facere ex hostibus.
   sed ubi Artotrogus hic est?   AR.   stat propter
                                              uirum
10 fortem atque fortunatam et forma regia;
   tum bellatorem—Mars haud ausit dicere
   neque aequiperare suas uirtutes ad tuas.
   PY. quemne ego seruaui in campis Curculioneis,
   ubi Bumbomachides Clutomestoridysarchides
15 erat imperator summus, Neptuni nepos?
   AR. memini. nempe illum dicis cum armis aureis,
   quoius tu legiones difflauisti spiritu,
   quasi uentus folia aut paniculum tectorium.
   PY. istuc quidem edepol nihil est.   AR.   nihil hercle
                                              hoc quidemst
20 praeut alia dicam—quae tu nunquam feceris.
   peiiuriorem hoc hominem si quis uiderit
   aut gloriarum pleniorem quam illic est,
   me sibi habeto, ego me mancupio dabo;
   nisi unum, epityra estur insanum bene.
25 PY. ubi tu es?   AR. eccum. edepol uel elephanto in
                                              India,
   quo pacto ei pugno praefregisti bracchium.
   PY. quid, 'bracchium'?   AR. illud dicere uolui,
                                              'femur.'
   PY. at indiligenter iceram.   AR. pol si quidem
   conixus esses, per corium, per uiscera
30 perque os elephanti transmineret bracchium.
   PY. nolo istaec hic nunc.   AR. ne hercle operae pre-
                                              tium quidemst
   mihi te narrare tuas qui uirtutes sciam.
   uenter creat omnis hasce aerumnas: auribus
   peraudienda sunt, ne dentes dentiant,
35 et adsentandumst quidquid hic mentibitur.

Py. quid illuc quod dico?   Ar. ehem, scio iam quid
uis dicere.
factum herclest, memini fieri.   Py. quid id est?   Ar.
quidquid est.
Py. habes— Ar. tabellas uis rogare. habeo, et stilum.
Py. facete aduortis tuom animum ad animum meum.
40 Ar. nouisse mores tuos me meditate decet
curamque adhibere ut praeolat mihi quod tu uelis.
Py. ecquid meministi?   Ar. memini centum in Cilicia
et quinquaginta, centum in Scytholatronia,
triginta Sardeis, sexaginta Macedones—
45 sunt homines quos tu—occidisti uno die.
Py. quanta istaec hominum summast?   Ar. septem
milia.
Py. tantum esse oportet. recte rationem tenes.
Ar. at nullos habeo scriptos: sic memini tamen.
Py. edepol memoria's optuma.   Ar. offae monent.
50 Py. dum tale facies quale adhuc, adsiduo edes,
communicabo semper te mensa mea.
Ar. quid in Cappadocia, ubi tu quingentos simul,
ni hebes machaera foret, uno ictu occideras?
Py. at peditastelli quia erant, siui uiuerent.
55 Ar. quid tibi ego dicam, quod omnes mortales sciunt,
Pyrgopolinicem te unum in terra uiuere
uirtute et forma et factis inuictissumum?

IV

The Shipwreck

(*Rudens*, ll. 160–289)

[Daemones and his slave Sceparnio watch from the
sea-shore the exciting escape of two young girls, Palaestra
and her serving-maid Ampelisca, from a ship wrecked
some way out at sea. The girls, after being separated in

the confusion of their landing in the rough surf, and after
wandering for some time in search of each other, meet,
and, in their lonely and sorry plight, beg assistance from
the priestess of the temple of Venus. The dramatic ending
(not cited here) to this play is that Palaestra is found to
be the long-lost daughter of Daemones.]

SCENE I

SCEPARNIO   DAEMONES

Sc. Sed, o Palaemo, sancte Neptuni comes,
qui Herculei socius esse diceris,
quod facinus uideo! DA. quid uides? Sc. mulierculas
uideo sedentis in scapha solas duas.
5 ut adflictantur miserae! eugae eugae, perbene!
ab saxo auortit fluctus ad litus scapham
neque gubernator umquam potuit tam bene.
non uidisse undas me maiores censeo.
saluae sunt si illos fluctus deuitauerint.
10 nunc, nunc periclumst. unda eiecit alteram.
at in uadost, iam facile enabit. eugepae!
uiden alteram illam ut fluctus eiecit foras?
surrexit, horsum se capessit. salua res.
desiluit haec autem altera in terram e scapha.
15 ut prae timore in genua in undas concidit!
saluast, euasit ex aqua. iam in litore est.
sed dextrouorsum auorsa it in malam crucem.
hem! errabit illaec hodie! DA. quid id refert
                                              tua?
Sc. si ad saxum quo capessit ea deorsum cadet,
20 errationis fecerit compendium.
DA. si tu de illarum cenaturus uesperi es,
illis curandum censeo, Sceparnio;
si apud med essuru's, mihi dari operam uolo.
Sc. bonum aequomque oras. DA. sequere me hac
                                      ergo.—Sc. sequor.—

SCENE II

Palaestra

Nimio hominum fortunae minus miserae memorantur
   quam in usu, experiundo is datur acerbum.
satin hoc deo complacitumst, med hoc ornatu ornatam
   in incertas regiones timidam eiectam?
5   hancine ego ad rem natam miseram me memorabo?
                                                    han-
   -cine ego partem capio ob pietatem praecipuam?
   nam hoc mi sat laborist laborem hunc potiri,
   si erga parentem aut deos me inpiaui;
   sed id si parate curaui ut cauerem,
10   tum hoc mi indecore, inique, inmodeste
   dati' di; nam quid habebunt sibi signi inpii posthac,
si ad hunc modum est innoxiis honor apud uos?
                     nam me si sciam
   fecisse aut parentes sceleste, minus me miserer;
15 sed erile scelus me sollicitat, eiius me inpietas male
                                                    habet.
      is nauem atque omnia perdidit in mari:
   haec bonorum eiiu' sunt reliquiae; etiam quae simul
   uecta mecum in scaphast excidit. ego nunc sola sum.
      quae mihi si foret salua saltem, labor
20   lenior esset hic mi eiius opera.
   nunc quam spem aut opem aut consili quid capes-
                                                    sam?
      ita hic sola solis locis compotita.
      hic saxa sunt, hic mare sonat,
      neque quisquam homo mi obuiam uenit.
25   hoc quod induta sum, summae opes oppido,
      nec cibo nec loco tecta quo sim scio:
      quae mihist spes qua me uiuere uelim?
      nec loci gnara sum nec uidi aut hic fui.
      saltem aliquem uelim qui mihi ex his locis

30   aut uiam aut semitam monstret, ita nunc
        hac an illac eam incerta sum consili;
        nec prope usquam hic quidem cultum agrum
                                        conspicor.
        algor, error, pauor, me omnia tenent.
        haec parentes mei hau sciti' miseri
35   me nunc miseram esse ita uti sum:
        leibera ego prognata fui maxume, nequiquam fui.
        nunc qui minu' seruio quasi serua forem nata?
        neque quicquam unquam illis profuit qui me sibi
                                        eduxerunt.

SCENE III

AMPELISCA   PALAESTRA

AM. Quid mihi meliust, quid magis in remst, quam a
                        corpore uitam ut secludam?
ita male uiuo atque ita mihi multae in pectore sunt
                        curae exanimales.
ita res se habent: uitae hau parco, perdidi spem qua
                        me oblectabam.
omnia iam circumcursaui atque omnibu' latebris per-
                                        reptaui
5 quaerere conseruam, uoce, oculis, auribus ut peruesti-
                                        garem.
neque eam usquam inuenio neque quo eam neque qua
                        quaeram consultumst,
neque quem rogitem responsorem quemquam interea
                        conuenio,
neque magi' solae terrae solae sunt quam haec loca
                        atque hae regiones;
neque, si uiuit, eam uiua unquam quin inueniam de-
                                        sistam.
10   PA. quoianam uox mihi
            prope hic sonat?
        AM. pertimui, quis hic loquitur prope?

PA. Spes bona, opsecro,
subuenta mihi.

15   AM. eximes ex hoc miseram metu?
PA. certo uox muliebris auris tetigit meas.
AM. mulier est, muliebris uox mi ad auris uenit.
PA. num Ampelisca opsecrost?   AM. ten, Palaestra,
audio?
PA. quin uoco ut me audiat nomine illam suo?
20 Ampelisca!   AM. hem quis est?   PA. ego Palaestra.
AM. dic ubi es?   PA. pol ego nunc in malis plurumis.
AM. socia sum nec minor pars meast quam tua.
sed uidere expeto te.   PA. mihi es aemula.
AM. consequamur gradu uocem. ubi es?   PA. ecce
me.
25 accede ad me atque adi contra.   AM. fit sedulo.
PA. cedo manum.   AM. accipe.   PA. dic, uiuisne?
opsecro.
AM. tu facis me quidem uiuere ut nunc uelim,
quom mihi te licet tangere. ut uix mihi
credo ego hoc, te tenere! opsecro, amplectere,
30 spes mea. ut me omnium iam laborum leuas.
PA. occupas praeloqui quae mea oratiost.
nunc abire hinc decet nos.   AM. quo, amabo,
ibimus?
PA. litus hoc persequamur.   AM. sequor quo lubet.
sicine hic cum uuida ueste grassabimur?
35 PA. hoc quod est, id necessarium est perpeti.
sed quid hoc, opsecro, est?   AM. quid?   PA. uiden,
amabo,
fanum hoc?   AM. ubi est?   PA. ad dexteram.
AM. uideo decorum dis locum uiderier.
PA. hau longe abesse oportet homines hinc, ita hic
lepidust locus.
40 quisquis est deu', ueneror ut nos ex hac aerumna
eximat,
miseras, inopes, aerumnosas ut aliquo auxilio adiuuet.

SCENE IV

PTOLEMOCRATIA   PALAESTRA   AMPELISCA

PT. Qui sunt qui a patrona preces mea expetessunt?
nam uox me precantum huc foras excitauit.
bonam atque opsequentem deam atque hau grauatam
patronam exsequontur benignamque multum.
5 PA. iubemus te saluere, mater.   PT. saluete,
            puellae. sed und' uos
      ire cum uuida ueste dicam, opsecro,
            tam maestiter uestitas?
PA. ilico hinc imus, hau longule ex hoc loco;
10 uerum longe hinc abest unde aduectae huc sumus.
   PT. nempe equo ligneo per uias caerulas
      estis uectae?   PA. admodum.   PT. ergo aequius uos
                                             erat
      candidatas uenire hostiatasque: ad hoc
      fanum ad istunc modum non ueniri solet.
15   PA. quaene eiectae e mari simus ambae, opsecro,
      unde nos hostias agere uoluisti huc?
      nunc tibi amplectimur genua egentes opum,
      quae in locis nesciis nescia spe sumus,
      ut tuo recipias tecto seruesque nos
20   miseriarumque te ambarum uti misereat,
      quibus nec locust ullus nec spes parata,
      neque hoc amplius quod uides nobis quicquamst.
   PT. manus mi date, exsurgite a genibus ambae.
   misericordior nulla me est feminarum.
25 sed haec pauperes res sunt inopes, puellae:
   egomet uix uitam colo; Ueneri cibo meo seruio.
         AM. Ueneris fanum, opsecro, hoc est?
      PT. fateor. ego huius fani sacerdos clueo.
      uerum quidquid est comiter fiet a me,
30   quo nunc copia ualebit.
      ite hac mecum.   PA. amice benigneque honorem,
      mater, nostrum habes.—PT. oportet.

V

The Twins

(Menaechmi, ll. 853–965)

[A merchant of Sicily had twin sons, one of whom was
stolen when still a child. The merchant having thereupon
died of a broken heart, the boys' grandfather re-named
the surviving son Menaechmus, after the child who was
stolen. This Menaechmus, on attaining manhood, travelled
in many countries in search of his lost brother (whom we
may call Menaechmus I), and came at last to Epidamnus,
where, as it happened, Menaechmus I had been brought
by the man who stole him, had married, and settled down
as a prominent and respected citizen. Menaechmus II
was, to his astonishment, hailed familiarly by many
people who took him for his twin brother, whom they
knew well, and, as may be readily imagined, numerous
complications ensued. In a chance interview between
Menaechmus II and the wife of Menaechmus I, who
naturally took the stranger for her husband, the former
became so enraged at the unaccountable attentions of the
woman he had never seen before, that the wife, on the
advice of her father, went for a doctor to cure her husband
of this supposed madness. In our first scene the prospective patient takes the hint, and by feigning madness
scares away his supposed father-in-law: he then slips off
from the scene of his embarrassment. In our second
scene, the doctor by mischance meets Menaechmus I,
who, returning home at this juncture, is in time to receive
professional advice for the disease with which his twin
is thought to be afflicted. It was not till chance
brought the twins face to face that proper explanations
could be made and a satisfactory ending given to the
story.]

SCENE I

MENAECHMUS II   SENEX

MEN. hau male illanc amoui; amoueam nunc hunc
　　　　　　　　　　　　　　inpurissumum.
ita mihi imperas ut ego huius membra atque ossa atque
　　　　　　　　　　　　　　artua
comminuam illo scipione quem ipse habet.   SE. dabitur
　　　　　　　　　　　　　　malum,
me quidem si attigeris aut si propius ad me accesseris.
5 MEN. faciam quod iubes; securim capiam ancipitem
　　　　　　　　　　　　atque hunc senem
osse tenus dolabo et concidam assulatim uiscera.
SE. enim uero illud praecauendumst atque adcuran-
　　　　　　　　　　　　　　dumst mihi;
sane ego illum metuo, ut minatur, ne quid male faxit
　　　　　　　　　　　　　　mihi.
MEN. multa mi imperas, Apollo: nunc equos iunctos
　　　　　　　　　　　　　　iubes
10 capere me indomitos, ferocis, atque in currum in-
　　　　　　　　　　　　　　scendere,
ut ego hunc proteram leonem uetulum, olentem, eden-
　　　　　　　　　　　　　　tulum.
iam astiti in currum, iam lora teneo, iam stimulum: in
　　　　　　　　　　　　　　manust.
agite equi, facitote sonitus ungularum appareat,
cursu celeri facite inflexa sit pedum pernicitas.
15 SE. mihin equis iunctis minare?   MEN. ecce, Apollo,
　　　　　　　　　　　　　　denuo
me iubes facere impetum in eum qui stat atque occidere.
sed quis hic est qui me capillo hinc de curru deripit?
imperium tuom demutat atque edictum Apollinis.
　　SE. eu hercle morbum acrem et durum.
20　　uel hic qui insanit quam ualuit paullo prius!

* Brix

    ei derepente tantus morbus incidit.
    eibo atque accersam medicum iam quantum potest.—
MEN. iamne isti abierunt, quaeso, ex conspectu meo,
qui me ui cogunt ut ualidus insaniam?
25 quid cesso abire ad nauem dum saluo licet?
    uosque omnis quaeso, si senex reuenerit,
    ni me indicetis qua platea hinc aufugerim.—
SE. lumbi sedendo, oculi spectando dolent,
    manendo medicum dum se ex opere recipiat.
30 odiosus tandem uix ab aegrotis uenit,
    ait se obligasse crus fractum Aesculapio,
    Apollini autem bracchium. nunc cogito
    utrum me dicam ducere medicum an fabrum.
    atque eccum incedit. moue formicinum gradum.

SCENE II

MEDICUS   SENEX   MENAECHMUS I

MED. quid esse illi morbi dixeras? narra, senex.
num laruatust aut cerritus? fac sciam.
num eum ueternus aut aqua intercus tenet?
SE. quin ea te caussa duco ut id dicas mihi
5 atque illum ut sanum facias.   MED. perfacile id
                              quidemst.
    sanum futurum, mea ego id promitto fide.
SE. magna cum cura ego illum curari uolo.
MED. quin suspirabo plus sescenta sexies,
    ita ego eum cum cura magna curabo tibi.
10 SE. atque eccum ipsum hominem. opseruemus quam
                             rem agat.
MEN. edepol ne hic dies peruorsus atque aduorsus mi
                             optigit.
quae me clam ratus sum facere, omnia ea fecit
                             palam
parasitus qui me compleuit flagiti et formidinis,
meus Ulixes, suo qui regi tantum conciuit mali.

15 quem ego hominem, si quidem uiuo, uita euoluam sua—
　　sed ego stultus sum, qui illius esse dico quae meast:
　　meo cibo et sumptu educatust. anima priuabo uirum.
　　SE. audin quae loquitur? MED. se miserum praedicat.
　　　　　　　　　　　　　　　　　　SE. adeas uelim.
　　MED. saluos sis, Menaechme. quaeso, qur apertas
　　　　　　　　　　　　　　　　　　　bracchium?
20 non tu scis quantum isti morbo nunc tuo facias mali?
　　MEN. quin tu te suspendis? SE. ecquid sentis? MED.
　　　　　　　　　　　　　　　　　quidni sentiam?
　　non potest haec res ellebori iungere optinerier.
　　sed quid ais, Menaechme? MEN. quid uis? MED. dic
　　　　　　　　　　　　　　mihi hoc quod te rogo.
　　album an atrum uinum potas? MEN. quin tu is in
　　　　　　　　　　　　　　　　malam crucem?
25 MED. iam hercle occeptat insanire primulum. MEN.
　　　　　　　　　　　　　　quin me interrogas
　　purpureum panem an puniceum soleam ego esse an
　　　　　　　　　　　　　　　　　luteum?
　　soleamne esse auis squamossas, piscis pennatos? SE.
　　　　　　　　　　　　　　　　　papae!
　　audin tu ut deliramenta loquitur? quid cessas dare
　　potionis aliquid priu' quam percipit insania?
30 MED. mane modo, etiam percontabor alia. SE. occidis
　　　　　　　　　　　　　　　　fabulans.
　　MED. dic mihi hoc: solent tibi umquam oculi duri
　　　　　　　　　　　　　　　　　fieri?
　　MEN. quid? tu me locustam censes esse, homo igna-
　　　　　　　　　　　　　　　　uissume?
　　MED. hoc quidem edepol hau pro insano uerbum re-
　　　　　　　　　　　　　　　spondit mihi.
　　perdormiscin usque ad lucem? facilin tu dormis cubans?
35 MEN. perdormisco, si resolui argentum quoi debeo—
　　qui te Iuppiter dique omnes, percontator, perduint!
　　MED. nunc homo insanire occeptat: de illis uerbis caue
　　　　　　　　　　　　　　　　　tibi.

SE. immo Nestor nunc quidem est de uerbis, praeut
          dudum fuit;
 nam dudum uxorem suam esse aiebat rabiosam canem.
40 MEN. quid, ego? SE. dixti insanus, inquam. MEN.
        egone? SE. tu istic, qui mihi
 etiam me iunctis quadrigis minitatu's prosternere.
 egomet haec te uidi facere, egomet haec ted arguo.
 MEN. at ego te sacram coronam surrupuisse Ioui'
           scio,
 et ob eam rem in carcerem ted esse compactum scio,
45 et postquam es emissus, caesum uirgis sub furca scio;
 tum patrem occidisse et matrem uendidisse etiam scio.
 satin haec pro sano male dicta male dictis respondeo?
 SE. opsecro hercle, medice, propere quidquid facturu's
           face.
 non uides hominem insanire? MED. scin quid facias
         optumum est?
50 ad me face uti deferatur. SE. itane censes? MED.
         quippini?
 ibi meo arbitratu potero curare hominem. SE. age ut
          lubet.
 MED. elleborum potabis faxo aliquos uiginti dies.
 MEN. at ego te pendentem fodiam stimulis triginta
          dies.
 MED. i, arcesse homines qui illunc ad me deferant.
        SE. quot sunt satis?
55 MED. proinde ut insanire uideo, quattuor, nihilo minus.
 SE. iam hic erunt. adserua tu istunc, medice. MED.
        immo ibo domum,
 ut parentur quibu' paratis opus est. tu seruos iube
 hunc ad me ferant. SE. iam ego illic faxo erit. MED.
        abeo.— SE. uale.—
 MEN. abiit socerus, abiit medicus. nunc solus sum.
        pro Iuppiter!
60 quid illuc est quod med hisce homines insanire prae-
         dicant?

nam equidem, postquam gnatus sum, numquam aegro-
taui unum diem
neque ego insanio neque pugnas neque ego litis coepio.
saluos saluos alios uideo, noui ego homines, adloquor.
an illi perperam insanire me aiunt, ipsi insaniunt?
65 quid ego nunc faciam? domum ire cupio: uxor non sinit;
huc autem nemo intromittit. nimi' prouentum est ne-
quiter.
hic ero usque: ad noctem saltem, credo, intromittar
domum.

VI

The Miser

(*Aulularia*, ll. 40–119, 406–472)

[Euclio was a harsh, crabbed old miser of Athens, who
kept buried in his house a large pot of gold. His efforts
to keep this treasure safe and unknown to his neighbours,
became a perfect mania with him. Our first scene shows
how he suspected everyone, even his faithful old servant
Staphyla, of secret designs for stealing his riches. He was
of course intensely anxious that people should think him
very poor, and in response to this wish, on the occasion
of his daughter's marriage, the bridegroom obligingly
provided a cook to prepare the wedding-feast. The warm
reception afforded by the ever-suspicious miser to this
stranger-menial, is set forth in our second extract.]

SCENE I

EUCLIO   STAPHYLA

EUC. Exi, inquam, age exi: exeundum hercle tibi hinc
est foras,
circumspectatrix cum oculis emissiciis.
STA. nam qur me miseram uerberas? EUC. ut misera sis,
atque ut te dignam mala malam aetatem exigas.

5 STA. nam qua me nunc caussa extrusisti ex aedibus?
EUC. tibi ego rationem reddam, stimulorum seges?
illuc regredere ab ostio. illuc sis uide,
ut incedit. at scin quo modo tibi res se habet?
si hercle hodie fustem cepero aut stimulum in manum,
10 testudineum istum tibi ego grandibo gradum.
STA. utinam me diui adaxint ad suspendium
potius quidem quam hoc pacto apud te seruiam.
EUC. at ut scelesta sola secum murmurat!
oculos hercle ego istos, inproba, ecfodiam tibi,
15 ne me opseruare possis quid rerum geram.
apscede etiam nunc—etiam nunc—etiam, ohe,
istic astato. si hercle tu ex istoc loco
digitum transuorsum aut unguem latum excesseris
aut si respexis, donicum ego te iussero,
20 continuo hercle ego te dedam discipulam cruci.
scelestiorem me hac anu certo scio
uidisse nunquam, nimi'que ego hanc metuo male
ne mi ex insidiis uerba inprudenti duit
neu persentiscat aurum ubi est apsconditum,
25 quae in occipitio quoque habet oculos pessuma.
nunc ibo ut uisam, estne ita aurum ut condidi,
quod me sollicitat plurumis miserum modis.—
STA. noenum mecastor quid ego ero dicam meo
malae rei euenisse quamue insaniam
30 queo comminisci; ita me miseram ad hunc modum
deciens die uno saepe extrudit aedibus.
nescio pol quae illunc hominem intemperiae tenent:
peruigilat noctes totas, tum autem interdius
quasi claudus sutor domi sedet totos dies.
35 EUC. nunc defaecato demum animo egredior domo,
postquam perspexi salua esse intus omnia.
redi nunciam intro atque intus serua. STA. quippini?
ego intus seruem? an ne quis aedis auferat?
nam hic apud nos nihil est aliud quaesti furibus,
40 ita inaniis sunt oppletae atque araneis.

Euc. mirum quin tua me caussa faciat Iuppiter
Philippum regem aut Dareum, triuenefica.
araneas mi ego illas seruari uolo.
pauper sum; fateor, patior; quod di dant fero.
45 abi intro, occlude ianuam. iam ego hic ero.
caue quemquam alienum in aedis intro miseris.
quod quispiam ignem quaerat, exstingui uolo,
ne caussae quid sit quod te quisquam quaeritet.
nam si ignis uiuet, tu exstinguere extempulo.
50 tum aquam aufugisse dicito, si quis petet.
cultrum, securim, pistillum, mortarium,
quae utenda uasa semper uicini rogant,
fures uenisse atque apstulisse dicito.
profecto in aedis meas me apsente neminem
55 uolo intro mitti. atque etiam hoc praedico tibi,
si Bona Fortuna ueniat, ne intro miseris.
Sta. pol ea ipsa credo ne intro mittatur cauet,
nam ad aedis nostras nusquam adiit quaquam prope.
Euc. tace atque abi intro. Sta. taceo atque abeo.—
                                    Euc. occlude sis
60 fores ambobus pessulis. iam ego hic ero.
discrucior animi, quia ab domo abeundum est mihi.
nimis hercle inuitus abeo. sed quid agam scio.
nam noster nostrae qui est magister curiae
diuidere argenti dixit nummos in uiros;
65 id si relinquo ac non peto, omnes ilico
me suspicentur, credo, habere aurum domi.
nam ueri simile non est hominem pauperem
pauxillum parui facere quin nummum petat.
nam nunc quom celo sedulo omnis ne sciant,
70 omnes uidentur scire et me benignius
omnes salutant quam salutabant prius;
adeunt, consistunt, copulantur dexteras,
rogitant me ut ualeam, quid agam, quid rerum geram.
nunc quo profectus sum ibo; postidea domum
75 me rusum quantum potero tantum recipiam.

SCENE II

CONGRIO   EUCLIO

Co. Attatae! ciues, populares, incolae, accolae, ad-
        uenae omnes,
date uiam qua fugere liceat, facite totae plateae pateant.
neque ego umquam nisi hodie ad Bacchas ueni in
        bacchanal coquinatum,
ita me miserum et meos discipulos fustibus male con-
        tuderunt.
5 totus doleo atque oppido perii, ita me iste habuit senex
        gymnasium;
        attat, perii hercle ego miser,
        aperit bacchanal, adest,
        sequitur. scio quam rem geram: hoc
        ipsu' magister me docuit.
10 neque ligna ego usquam gentium praeberi uidi pul-
        chrius,
itaque omnis exegit foras, me atque hos, onustos
        fustibus.
Euc. redi. quo fugis nunc? tene, tene. Co. quid,
        stolide, clamas?
Euc. quia ad tresuiros iam ego deferam nomen tuom.
        Co. quam ob rem?
Euc. quia cultrum habes. Co. coquom decet. Euc.
        quid comminatu's
15 mihi? Co. istuc male factum arbitror, quia non latu'
        fodi.
Euc. homo nullust te scelestior qui uiuat hodie,
neque quoi ego de industria amplius male plus lubens
        faxim.
Co. pol etsi taceas, palam id quidem est: res ipsa
        testest;
ita fustibus sum mollior magi' quam ullu' cinaedus.
20 sed quid tibi nos tactiost, mendice homo? Euc. quae
        res?

etiam rogitas? an quia minus quam aequom erat
feci?
Co. sine, at hercle cum magno malo tuo, si hoc caput
sentit.
Euc. pol ego hau scio quid post fuat: tuom nunc
caput sentit.
sed in aedibus quid tibi meis nam erat negoti
25 me apsente, nisi ego iusseram? uolo scire. Co. tace
ergo.
quia uenimu' coctum ad nuptias. Euc. quid tu,
malum, curas
utrum crudum an coctum ego edim, nisi tu mi es
tutor?
Co. uolo scire, sinas an non sinas nos coquere hic
cenam?
Euc. uolo scire ego item, meae domi mean salua
futura?
30 Co. utinam mea mihi modo auferam, quae ad te tuli,
salua:
me hau paenitet, tua ne expetam. Euc. scio, ne doce,
noui.
Co. quid est qua prohibes nunc gratia nos coquere hic
cenam?
quid fecimus, quid diximus tibi secu' quam uelles?
Euc. etiam rogitas, sceleste homo, qui angulos omnis
35 mearum aedium et conclauium mihi peruium facitis?
ibi ubi tibi erat negotium, ad focum si adesses,
non fissile auferres caput: merito id tibi factum est.
adeo ut tu meam sententiam iam noscere possis:
si ad ianuam huc accesseris, nisi iussero, propius,
40 ego te faciam miserrumus mortalis uti sis.
scis iam meam sententiam.—Co. quo abis? redi
rusum.
ita me bene amet Lauerna, te iam iam, nisi reddi
mihi uasa iubes, pipulo te hic differam ante
aedis.

quid ego nunc agam? ne ego edepol ueni huc auspicio
　　　　　　　　　　　　　　　　　　　malo.
45 nummo sum conductus: plus iam medico mercedest
　　　　　　　　　　　　　　　　　　　opus.
　　Euc.　hoc quidem hercle, quoquo ibo, mecum erit,
　　　　　　　　　　　　　　　　　mecum feram,
　　neque istic in tantis periclis umquam committam ut
　　　　　　　　　　　　　　　　　　　siet.
　ite sane nunc intro omnes, et coqui et tibicinae,
　etiam intro duce, si uis, uel gregem uenalium,
50 coquite, facite, festinate nunciam quantum lubet.
　　Co.　temperi, postquam impleuisti fusti fissorum caput.
　　Euc.　intro abi: opera huc conducta est uostra, non
　　　　　　　　　　　　　　　　　oratio.
　　Co.　heus, senex, pro uapulando hercle ego aps te mer-
　　　　　　　　　　　　　　　　cedem petam.
　coctum ego, non uapulatum, dudum conductus fui.
55 Euc.　lege agito mecum. molestus ne sis. i cenam
　　　　　　　　　　　　　　　　　coque,
　　aut abi in malum cruciatum ab aedibus.　Co.　abi tu
　　　　　　　　　　　　　　　　　modo.—
　　Euc.　illic hinc abiit. di inmortales, facinus audax
　　　　　　　　　　　　　　　　　incipit
　qui cum opulento pauper homine rem habere aut
　　　　　　　　　　　　　　　　negotium.
　ueluti Megadorus temptat me omnibus miserum modis,
60 qui simulauit mei honoris mittere huc caussa coquos:
　is ea caussa misit, hoc qui surruperent misero mihi.
　condigne etiam meu' med intus gallus gallinacius,
　qui erat anui peculiaris, perdidit paenissume.
　ubi erat haec defossa, occepit ibi scalpurrire ungulis
65 circumcirca. quid opust uerbis? ita mi pectus peracuit:
　capio fustem, optrunco gallum, furem manifestarium.
　credo edepol ego illi mercedem gallo pollicitos coquos,
　si id palam fecisset. exemi ex manu manubrium.
　quid opust uerbis? facta est pugna in gallo gallinacio.

VII

The Parasite

(*Captiui*, ll. 126–194)

[In this scene the parasite Ergasilus has recourse to much ingenious flattery, in order to coax his patron Hegio to invite him to dinner. In particular he pretends to sympathise very strongly with the old man, who is greatly distressed because his son has been taken prisoner in a recent war.]

HEGIO   ERGASILUS

HE. Ego ibo ad fratrem ad alios captiuos meos,
uisam ne nocte hac quippiam turbauerint.
ind' me continuo recipiam rusum domum.
ER. aegre est mi hunc facere quaestum carcerarium
5 propter sui gnati miseriam miserum senem.
sed si ullo pacto ille huc conciliari potest,
uel carnuficinam hunc facere possum perpeti.
HE. quis hic loquitur?   ER. ego, qui tuo maerore
                            maceror.
macesco, consenesco, et tabesco miser;
10 ossa atque pellis sum misera—macritudine;
neque umquam quicquam me iuuat quod edo domi:
foris aliquantillum etiam quod gusto id beat.
HE. Ergasile, salue.   ER. di te bene ament, Hegio.
HE. ne fle.   ER. egone illum non fleam? ego non defleam
15 talem adulescentem?   HE. semper sensi filio
meo te esse amicum et illum intellexi tibi.
ER. tum denique homines nostra intellegimus bona,
quom quae in potestate habuimus ea amisimus.
ego, postquam gnatus tuo' potitust hostium,
20 expertus quanti fuerit nunc desidero.
HE. alienus quom eius incommodum tam aegre feras,
quid me patrem par facerest, quoi ille est unicus?

ER. alienus? ego alienus illi? aha, Hegio,
numquam istuc dixis neque animum induxis tuom;
25 tibi ille unicust, mi etiam unico magis unicus.
HE. laudo, malum quom amici tuom ducis malum.
nunc habe bonum animum.　ER. eheu, huic illud
　　　　　　　　　　　　　　　　　dolet,—
quia nunc remissus est edendi exercitus.
HE. nullumne interea nactu's, qui posset tibi
30 remissum quem dixti imperare exercitum?
ER. quid credis? fugitant omnes hanc prouinciam,
quoi optigerat postquam captust Philopolemus tuos.
HE. non pol mirandum est fugitare hanc prouinciam.
multis et multigeneribus opus est tibi
35 militibus: primumdum opus est Pistorensibus;
eorum sunt aliquot genera Pistorensium:
opu' Panicis est, opu' Placentinis quoque;
opu' Turdetanis, opust Ficedulensibus;
iam maritumi omnes milites opu' sunt tibi.
40 ER. ut saepe summa ingenia in occulto latent!
hic qualis imperator nunc priuatus est.
HE. habe modo bonum animum, nam illum confido
　　　　　　　　　　　　　　　　　domum
in his diebus me reconciliassere.
nam eccum hic captiuom adulescentem Aleum,
45 prognatum genere summo et summis ditiis:
hoc illum me mutare—— ER. confido fore.
ita di deaeque faxint. sed num quo foras
uocatus es ad cenam? HE. nusquam, quod sciam.
sed quid tu id quaeris? ER. quia mi est natalis dies;
50 propterea a te uocari ad te ad cenam uolo.
HE. facete dictum! sed si pauxillum potes
contentus esse. ER. ne perpauxillum modo,
nam istoc me adsiduo uictu delecto domi;
age sis, roga emptum: 'nisi qui meliorem adferet
55 quae mihi atque amicis placeat condicio magis,'
quasi fundum uendam, meis me addicam legibus.

He. profundum uendis tu quidem, hau fundum, mihi.
sed si uenturu's, temperi. Er. em, uel iam otium est.
He. i modo, uenare leporem: nunc ictim tenes;
60 nam meu' scruposam uictus commetat uiam.
Er. numquam istoc uinces me, Hegio, ne postules:
cum calceatis dentibus ueniam tamen.
He. asper meu' uictus sane est. Er. sentisne essitas?
He. terrestris cena est. Er. sus terrestris bestia est.
65 He. multis holeribus. Er. curato aegrotos domi.
numquid uis?   He. uenias temperi.   Er. memorem
                                                    mones.—
He. ibo intro atque intus subducam ratiunculam,
quantillum argenti mi apud tarpezitam siet.
ad fratrem, quo ire dixeram, mox iuero.

VIII

A Business Transaction
(*Asinaria*, ll. 332–503)

[In the first scene two slaves, Leonida and Libanus,
plan together to deceive a Macedonian merchant (Mercator) into paying them the money due to their master
on a sale of asses. In the two subsequent scenes they try
to put their plan into execution, but without success.]

SCENE I

Leonida   Libanus

Le. Animum aduorte, ut aeque mecum haec scias. Li.
                                                    taceo. Le. beas.
meministin asinos Arcadicos mercatori Pelleo
nostrum uendere atriensem? Li. memini. quid tum
                                                    postea?
Le. em ergo is argentum huc remisit quod daretur
                                                    Saureae

3–2

5 pro asinis. adulescens uenit modo, qui id argentum
attulit.

LI. ubi is homost? LE. iam deuorandum censes, si
conspexeris?

LI. ita enim uero. sed tamen tu nempe eos asinos
praedicas

uetulos, claudos, quibu' suptritae ad femina iam erant
ungulae?

LE. ipsos, qui tibi subuectabant rure huc uirgas ulmeas.

10 LI. teneo, atque idem te hinc uexerunt uinctum rus.
LE. memor es probe.

uerum in tostrina ut sedebam, me infit percontarier
ecquem filium Stratonis nouerim Demaenetum.
dico me nouisse extemplo et me eius seruom praedico
esse, et aedis demonstraui nostras. LI. quid tum
postea?

15 LE. ait se ob asinos ferre argentum atriensi Saureae,
uiginti minas, sed eum non nosse hominem qui siet,
ipsum uero se nouisse callide Demaenetum.
quoniam ille elocutus haec sic— LI. quid tum? LE.
ausculta ergo, scies.

extemplo facio facetum me atque magnuficum uirum,

20 dico med esse atriensem. sic hoc respondit mihi:
'ego pol Sauream non noui neque qua facie sit scio.
te non aequomst suscensere. si erum uis Demaenetum,
quam ego noui, adduce: argentum non morabor quin
feras.'

ego me dixeram adducturum et me domi praesto
fore;

25 ille in balineas iturust, inde huc ueniet postea.
quid nunc consili captandum censes? dice. LI. em
istuc ago

quo modo argento interuortam et aduentorem et
Sauream.

iam hoc opus est exasceato: nam si ille argentum prius
hospes huc adfert, continuo nos ambo exclusi sumus.

30 nam me hodie senex seduxit solum sorsum ab aedibus,
mihi tibique interminatust nos futuros ulmeos,
ni hodie Argyrippo argenti essent uiginti minae;
iussit uel nos atriensem uel nos uxorem suam
defrudare, dixit sese operam promiscam dare.
35 nunc tu abi ad forum ad erum et narra haec ut nos
acturi sumus:
te ex Leonida futurum esse atriensem Sauream,
dum argentum adferat mercator pro asinis. LE. faciam
ut iubes.
LI. ego illum interea hic oblectabo, priu' si forte ad-
uenerit.
LE. quid ais? LI. quid uis? LE. pugno malam si
tibi percussero,
40 mox quom Sauream imitabor, caueto ne suscenseas.
LI. hercle uero tu cauebis ne me attingas, si sapis,
ne hodie malo cum auspicio nomen commutaueris.
LE. quaeso, aequo animo patitor. LI. patitor tu item
quom ego te referiam.
LE. dico ut usust fieri. LI. dico hercle ego quoque ut
facturu' sum.
45 LE. ne nega. LI. quin promitto, inquam, hostire
contra ut merueris.
LE. ego abeo, tu iam, scio, patiere. sed quis hic est?
is est,
ille est ipsus. iam ego recurro huc. tu hunc interea hic
tene.
uolo seni narrare. LI. quin tuom officium facis ergo
ac fugis?

SCENE II

MERCATOR   LIBANUS

ME. ut demonstratae sunt mihi, hasce aedis esse
oportet
Demaenetus ubi dicitur habitare. i, puere, pulta
atque atriensem Sauream, si est intus, euocato huc.

Li. quis nostras sic frangit fores? ohe, inquam, si quid
audis.
5 Me. nemo etiam tetigit. sanun es?   Li. at censebam
attigisse
propterea huc quia habebas iter. nolo ego fores conseruas
meas a te uerberarier. sane ego sum amicus nostris.
Me. pol hau periclum est cardines ne foribus ecfrin-
gantur,
si istoc exemplo omnibus qui quaerunt respondebis.
10 Li. ita haec morata est ianua: extemplo ianitorem
clamat, procul si quem uidet ire ad se calcitronem.
sed quid uenis? quid quaeritas?   Me. Demaenetum
uolebam.
Li. si sit domi, dicam tibi.   Me. quid eius atriensis?
Li. nihilo mage intus est.   Me. ubi est?   Li. ad
tonsorem ire dixit.
15 Me. quom uenisset, post non redit?   Li. non edepol.
quid uolebas?
Me. argenti uiginti minas, si adesset, accepisset.
Li. qui pro istuc?   Me. asinos uendidit Pellaeo mercatori
mercatu.   Li. scio. tu id nunc refers? iam hic credo
eum adfuturum.
Me. qua facie uester Saurea est? si is est, iam scire
potero.
20 Li. macilentis malis, rufulus aliquantum, uentriosus,
truculentis oculis, commoda statura, tristi fronte.
Me. non potuit pictor rectius describere eiius formam.
Li. atque hercle ipsum adeo contuor, quassanti capite
incedit.
quisque obuiam huic occesserit irato, uapulabit.
25 Me. siquidem hercle Aeacidinis minis animisque ex-
pletus cedit.
si med iratus tetigerit, iratus uapulabit.

SCENE III

LEONIDA   MERCATOR   LIBANUS

LE. quid hoc sit negoti neminem meum dictum magni
facere?
Libanum in tostrinam ut iusseram uenire, is nullus
uenit.
ne ille edepol tergo et cruribus consuluit hau decore.
ME. nimis imperiosust. LI. uae mihi! LE. hodie
saluere iussi
5 Libanum libertum? iam manu emissu's? LI. obsecro
te.
LE. ne tu hercle cum magno malo mihi obuiam oc-
cessisti.
qur non uenisti, ut iusseram, in tostrinam? LI. hic
me moratust.
LE. siquidem hercle nunc summum Iouem te dicas
detinuisse
atque is precator adsiet, malam rem ecfugies nunquam.
10 tu, uerbero, imperium meum contempsisti? LI. perii,
hospes.
ME. quaeso, hercle, noli, Saurea, mea caussa hunc
uerberare.
LE. utinam nunc stimulus in manu mihi sit,— ME.
quiesce, quaeso.
LE. qui latera conteram tua, quae occalluere plagis.
apscede ac sine me hunc perdere, qui semper me ira
incendit,
15 quoi nunquam unam rem me licet semel praecipere furi,
quin centiens eadem imperem atque ogganniam, itaque
iam hercle
clamore ac stomacho non queo labori suppeditare.
iussin, sceleste, ab ianua hoc stercus hinc auferri?
iussin columnis deici operas araneorum?
20 iussin in splendorem dare bullas has foribus nostris?

nihil est: tanquam si claudu' sim, cum fustist ambu-
landum.

quia triduom hoc unum modo foro operam adsiduam
dedo,

dum reperiam qui quaeritet argentum in faenus, hic
uos

dormitis interea domi atque erus in hara, haud in
aedibus, habitat.

25 em ergo hoc tibi.   LI. hospes, te obsecro, defende.
ME. Saurea, oro

mea caussa ut mittas.   LE. eho, ecquis pro uectura
oliui

rem soluit?   LI. soluit.   LE. quoi datumst?   LI.
Sticho uicario ipsi

tuo.   LE. uah! delenire apparas, scio mi uicarium esse,
neque eo esse seruom in aedibus eri qui sit pluris quam
illest.

30 sed uina quae heri uendidi uinario Exaerambo,
iam pro eis sati' fecit Sticho?   LI. fecisse satis opinor,
nam uidi huc ipsum adducere tarpezitam Exaerambum.
LE. sic dedero.   priu' quae credidi, uix anno post exegi;
nunc sat agit: adducit domum etiam ultro et scribit
nummos.

35 Dromo mercedem rettulit?   LI. dimidio minus opinor.
LE. quid relicuom?   LI. aibat reddere quom extemplo
redditum esset;

nam retineri, ut quod sit sibi operis locatum ecficeret.
LE. scyphos quos utendos dedi Philodamo, rettulitne?
LI. non etiam.   LE. hem non? si uelis, da, commoda
homini amico.

40 ME. perii hercle, iam hic me abegerit suo odio.   LI.
heus iam satis tu.

audin quae loquitur?   LE. audio et quiesco.   ME.
tandem, opinor,

conticuit: nunc adeam optumum est, priu' quam incipit tinnire.

quam mox mi operam das? LE. ehem, optume. quam
                          dudum tu aduenisti?
non hercle te prouideram (quaeso, ne uitio uortas),
45 ita iracundia opstitit oculis. ME. non mirum factum
                              est.
sed si domi est, Demaenetum uolebam. LE. negat
                           esse intus.
uerum istuc argentum tamen mihi si uis denumerare,
repromittam istoc nomine solutam rem futuram.
ME. sic potius ut Demaeneto tibi ero praesente reddam.
50 LI. erus istunc nouit atque erum hic. ME. ero huic
                      praesente reddam.
LI. da modo meo periculo, rem saluam ego exhibebo;
nam si sciat noster senex fidem non esse huic habitam,
suscenseat, quoii omnium rerum ipsus semper credit.
LE. non magni pendo. ne duit, si non uolt. sic sine
                          astet.
55 LI. da, inquam. uah, formido miser ne hic me tibi
                      arbitretur
suasisse sibi ne crederes. da, quaeso, ac ne formida:
saluom hercle erit. ME. credam fore, dum quidem
                   ipse in manu habebo.
peregrinus ego sum, Sauream non noui. LI. at nosce
                       sane.
ME. sit, non sit, non edepol scio. si is est, eum esse
                      oportet.
60 ego certe me incerto scio hoc daturum nemini homini.
LE. hercle istum di omnes perduint. uerbo caue sup-
                    plicassis.
ferox est uiginti minas meas tractare sese.
nemo accipit, aufer te domum, apscede hinc, molestus
                    ne sis.
ME. nimis iracunde. non decet superbum esse hominem
                    seruom.
65 LE. malo hercle iam magno tuo, ni isti nec recte dicis.
LI. impure, nihili. non uideas irasci? LE. perge porro.

LI. flagitium hominis. da, opsecro, argentum huic, ne
                                 male loquatur.
ME. malum hercle uobis quaeritis.   LE. crura hercle
                                 diffringentur,
ni istum impudicum percies.   LI. perii hercle. age,
                                 inpudice,
70 sceleste, non audes mihi scelesto subuenire?
   LE. pergin precari pessumo?   ME. quae res? tun
                                 libero homini
male seruos loquere?   LE. uapula.   ME. id quidem
                                 tibi hercle fiet
ut uapules, Demaenetum simul ac conspexero hodie.
in ius uoco te.   LE. non eo.   ME. non is? memento.
                                 LE. memini.
75 ME. dabitur pol supplicium mihi de tergo uostro.   LE.
                                 uae te!
tibi quidem supplicium, carnufex, de nobis detur?
                                 ME. atque etiam
pro dictis uostris maledicis poenae pendentur mi hodie.
LE. quid, uerbero? ain tu, furcifer? erum nosmet
                                 fugitare censes?
i nunciam ad erum, quo uocas, iam dudum quo
                                 uolebas.
80 ME. nunc demum? tamen nunquam hinc feres ar-
                                 genti nummum, nisi me
dare iusserit Demaenetus.   LE. ita facito, age ambula
                                 ergo.
tu contumeliam alteri facias, tibi non dicatur?
tam ego homo sum quam tu.   ME. scilicet. ita res
                                 est.   LE. sequere hac ergo.
praefiscini hoc nunc dixerim: nemo etiam me accusauit
85 merito meo, neque me Athenis alter est hodie quisquam
quoi credi recte aeque putent.   ME. fortassis. sed
                                 tamen me
nunquam hodie induces ut tibi credam hoc argentum
                                 ignoto.

lupus est homo homini, non homo, quom qualis sit non
                                                nouit.
LE. iam nunc secunda mihi facis. scibam huic te
                                          capitulo hodie
90 facturum sati' pro iniuria; quamquam ego sum sor-
                                                didatus,
frugi tamen sum, nec potest peculium enumerari.
ME. fortasse. LE. etiam nunc dico Periphanes Rhodo
                                          mercator diues
apsente ero solus mihi talentum argenti soli
adnumerauit et credidit mihi, neque deceptust in eo.
95 ME. fortasse. LE. atque etiam tu quoque ipse, si
                                          esses percontatus
me ex aliis, scio pol crederes nunc quod fers. ME. hau
                                                negassim.

IX

The Carthaginian
(*Poenulus*, ll. 53–128)

[The extract from this play is from the Prologue, which
was recited on the stage before the beginning of the play,
in order that the audience might be instructed in a general
outline of the plot. This extract, then, describes the
adventures of Hanno, a Carthaginian, as they are to be
reproduced upon the stage.]

SCENE I

PROLOGUE

Καρχηδόνιος uocatur haec comoedia;
latine Plautus 'Patruos Pultiphagonides.'
nomen iam habetis. nunc rationes ceteras
accipite: nam argumentum hoc hic censebitur:

5 locus argumentost suom sibi proscaenium,
uos iuratores estis. quaeso, operam date.
Carthaginienses fratres patrueles duo
fuere summo genere et summis ditiis;
eorum alter uiuit, alter est emortuos.
10 propterea apud uos dico confidentius,
quia mi pollictor dixit qui eum pollinxerat.
sed illi seni qui mortuost, ei filius
unicu' qui fuerat ab diuitiis a patre
puer septuennis surrupitur Carthagine,
15 sexennio priu' quidem quam moritur pater.
quoniam periisse sibi uidet gnatum unicum,
conicitur ipse in morbum ex aegritudine:
facit illum heredem fratrem patruelem suom,
ipse abit ad Accheruntem sine uiatico.
20 ill' qui surrupuit puerum Calydonem auehit,
uendit eum domino hic diuiti quoidam seni,
cupienti liberorum, osori mulierum.
emit hospitalem is filium imprudens senex
puerum illum eumque adoptat sibi pro filio
25 eumque heredem fecit quom ipse obiit diem.
is illic adulescens habitat in illisce aedibus.
reuortor rusus denuo Carthaginem:
siquid amandare uoltis aut curarier,
argentum nisi qui dederit, nugas egerit;
30 uerum qui dederit, magi' maiores egerit.
sed illi patruo huiius qui uiuit senex,
Carthaginiensi duae fuere filiae,
altera quinquennis, altera quadrimula:
cum nutrice una periere a Magaribus.
35 eas qui surrupuit in Anactorium deuehit,
uendit eas omnis, et nutricem et uirgines,
praesenti argento homini.
is ex Anactorio, ubi prius habitauerat,
huc in Calydonem commigrauit hau diu,
40 sui quaesti caussa. is in illis habitat aedibus.

earum hic adulescens alteram ecflictim perit,
suam sibi cognatam, inprudens, neque scit quae siet.
sed pater illarum Poenus, posquam eas perdidit,
mari terraque usquequaque quaeritat.
45 ubi quamque in urbem est ingressus, ilico
omnis puellas, ubi quisque habitant, inuenit:
rogitat postibi
und' sit, quoiatis, captane an surrupta sit,
quo genere nata, qui parentes fuerint.
50 ita docte atque astu filias quaerit suas.
et is omnis linguas scit, sed dissimulat sciens
se scire: Poenus plane est. quid uerbis opust?
is heri huc in portum naui uenit uesperi,
pater harunc: idem huic patruos adulescentulo est:
55 iamne hoc tenetis? si tenetis, ducite;
caue dirrumpatis, quaeso, sinite transigi.
ehem, paene oblitus sum relicuom dicere.
ill' qui adoptauit hunc sibi pro filio,
is illi Poeno huius patruo hospes fuit.
60 hic qui hodie ueniet reperiet suas filias
et hunc sui fratris filium. dehinc ceterum
ualete, adeste. ibo, alius nunc fieri uolo:
quod restat, restant alii qui faciant palam.
ualete atque ut uos seruet Salus.

NOTES

I

A Strange Dilemma

Scene I

1. **edepol,** literally "by Pollux," hence "indeed, truly." For the formation of this word cf. *ecastor,* "by Castor."

ubi terrarum, "where on earth" (partitive genitive).

2. **miser,** "wretched that I am."

3. **ilicet** (contracted from *ire-licet*), "It is all over." This was the phrase used by the court-crier to the jury at the dismissal of a law-suit.

una et, "together with."

4. **certumst** = *certum est,* "I am resolved." Elision of *m* and *s* is frequent in Plautus; cf. in this scene, l. 8 *seruo'sne = seruos es-ne,* and l. 46 *erust = erus est.*

contra, always an adverb in Plautus.

conloqui ("to speak with") is often used with a direct object in Plautus; cf. l. 898 of this play, *te uolo, uxor, conloqui.* In later Latin it is most commonly constructed with *cum aliquo* and *inter se.*

5. **qui,** an old ablative grown into a conjunction, and equivalent to *quo, ut.* Cf. "The Shipwreck," sc. ii, l. 37.

6. **Volcanum,** the god of fire, used metaphorically for fire itself. Cf. *Aeneid* VII, 77 *totis Volcanum spargere tectis.* Similarly, *Ceres* is used for bread, and *Bacchus* for wine.

cornu, lanterns were made of horn in ancient times. Cf. Lucr. II, 388 *lumen per cornum transit.* Until recently our own word "lantern" was popularly spelt "lanthorn," in supposed allusion to the horn which formed the sides of our early lanterns.

geris, "carry."

7. **pugnis,** from *pugnus,* "a fist."

exossas, from *ex* and *ŏs,* literally "to deprive of bones." Note the jingle with the preceding *ŏs.*

8. **seruos,** old form of nominative singular *seruus;* very frequent in Plautus, cf. l. 44 *uaniloquos,* and l. 63 *uiuos.*

9. **uerbero.** Mercury uses this word as a noun, meaning "a rascal" (literally, "one worthy of a flogging"). Sosia pretends to think that he uses it as a verb, "I am flogging" (from *uerberare*), and accuses him of a lie. Mercury, by way of a retort, threatens to make his words come true by flogging Sosia. Tr. "'Igh time you were whipped!" " *You* time? You're a liar."

10. Construe, *faciam ut dicas* [*me*] *uerum dicere.*

11. **quoius** = *cuius*, masculine nominative singular of interrogative pronoun. See "The Shipwreck," sc. iii, l. 10, note. (Similarly *quoi* = *cui*.) **Quoius sis** (dependent question) = "to whom you belong."

12. **es certior,** not to be translated as a comparative; cf. the familiar phrase *certiorem facere,* "to inform."

13. **hodie,** see note on l. 91.

tibi, dative of interest.

14. **pergin** = *pergisne.*

argutarier (old infinitive) = *argutari,* "to chatter," in the main an ante-classical word, used only by Propertius among later writers.

15. **negoti** = *negotii,* partitive genitive dependent on *quid,* "what business."

16. **Creo,** the king of Thebes. **uigiles,** "sentries."

17. **quia,** see note on "The Parasite," l. 28.

tutatust = *tutatus est* (deponent), "kept guard."

18. **familiaris** (plural), "family servants." Mercury puns on this, two lines below, in the word *familiariter,* "familiarly"; a literal translation of the pun holds good in English.

19. **actutum,** see note on sc. ii, l. 84.

20. **faxo,** archaic future of *facio.* (Similarly *faxim* is its present subjunctive.) **Accipiere** = *accipieris,* dependent on *faxo.*

21. **at scin quo modo?** (*scin* = *scis-ne*). This is a common formula in Plautus, and is generally used for threats. "Now then."

22. **superbum,** usually "proud," here a pun on the literal meaning of *super,* from which it is derived. Translate, "exalted." It is explained in the next line, where Mercury says he will cudgel Sosia until he has to be carried out instead of being able to walk of his own accord.

24. **quin,** remonstrating, "oh, but."

25. **uapulare.** This verb, though active in form, is passive in meaning, "to be flogged."

sis = *si uis,* "if you please."

26. **tun** = *tu-ne.*

postulas, "want," governing *prohibere.*

28. **praefectust legionibus,** "is commander of the legion."

Note that the Roman technical term *legio* is used frequently in this scene, although the story was originally Greek.

29. **quicum.** *Qui* is again an old ablative.

quid ais, a common Plautine colloquialism, "I say."

30. **uocant,** sc. *me*, with which *prognatum* agrees.

Dauo, ablative of origin.

32. **audaciai,** old form of genitive *audaciae*.

columen, old form of *culmen*; "crown of impudence."

consutis, literally, "patched up." Translate this pun by "a tissue of lies," and "a tissue of good cloth." (Palmer.)

34. **etiam,** often used, as here, by Plautus in expostulations.

35. **ita profecto,** "yes indeed." Sosia owns the obvious truth of Mercury's retort.

36. **ingratiis,** "whether you will or no." (*Gratiis* in Plautus means "for nothing.")

37. **certum,** "a certainty"; **arbitrarium,** "a matter of opinion." This distinction between *certus* and *arbitrarius* was recognised in the judicial language of the day.

38. Construe *tu-ne audes dicere te esse Sosiam?*

39. **perii,** "I am undone."

praeut, "in comparison with." In view of the flogging Sosia is going to get, Mercury thinks that *perii* understates the case.

40. **pugnis usu fecisti tuom,** "you have established a claim to me by your fists," literally, "by means of your fists you have made me yours by the 'use that creates ownership.'" For this meaning of the word *usus* cf. Cicero, *hereditas usu capta,* "an inheritance of which the ownership had been acquired by long use."

41. **pro fidem!** "Help, help!" This *pro* (sometimes, but less correctly, written *proh*) is not a preposition, but an interjection expressing wonder or lamentation. It can be used (1) with the nominative (e.g. *pro Iuppiter!*); (2) by itself (e.g. in Livy, *tantum, pro! degeneramus a patribus*); (3), as here, with the accusative; (4) very rarely with the genitive.

42. **ut esset quem...,** "so that you should have some one to...."

48. **peccaueram,** "I made a mistake." This use of the pluperfect is common in Plautus. Cf. the last line of our extract from the *Captiui—ad fratrem, quo ire dixeram, mox iuero.*

49. **socium,** a pun on the name *Sosia*, the pronunciation of both words being presumably somewhat alike. Tr. "associate."

ne, see note on "The Twins," sc. ii, l. 11.

51. **istuc fecissent,** i.e. *me fugissent*, from the last sentence.

52. **dudum,** see note on sc. ii, l. 59.

56. **fide,** old dative.

57. **siet** = *sit*. This is really an optative form like εἴην, the original (though obsolete) form of which must have been ἐσίην, as *siem* was originally *esiem*. The *ie* is contracted to *i* in *sim* and in the other subjunctives in *-im*, e.g. *uelim, edim*.

59. **etiam denuo?** "what, again?" *Denuo* is contracted from *de nŏuo*, which never actually occurs.

64. **alieno,** "to make one person into another"—its original meaning.

67. Construe *id uitium, quod mihi praedicas, tibi est*.

68. **quid, malum,** "what, plague take it!"

70. **quae,** refers back to *nauis*.

73. **mālae,** "jaws," to be distinguished from *mălae*.

78. **ubi** depends on *oppidum*, "the town in which."

80. **ipsus** = *ipse*. This old form is found in Plautus, Cato and Terence.

82. **memorat memoriter.** Note the jingle of words. *Memoriter* means "with good memory," not "from memory."

84. **qui,** old ablative, = *qua* (of which the antecedent is *patera*, the subject of the sentence, in reply to the question *quid est datum?*).

potitare, "to drink often," a Plautine word, a frequentative form of *potare*.

86. **signi,** a partitive genitive dependent on *quid*.

87. **quid me captas?** "why are you trying to catch me tripping?"

89. **nescio unde,** to be regarded as forming together a single word, like *nescioquis*. Hence the indicative *spectauit*.

90. **nec...adfuit,** must be treated as being in a bracket; otherwise it confuses the construction of the whole sentence.

91. **hodie,** not to be translated "to-day," but used here, as frequently in Plautus, pleonastically, to strengthen the negative ("at all"). Cf. Verg. *Ecl.* iii, 49 *nunquam hodie effugies*.

94. **ingressust uiam,** "he's begun," i.e. to say exactly what happened.

95. **uini meri.** The genitive depends on *eduxi* in the sense of "make empty of."

98. **argumentis,** not "by arguments" but "by proofs."

99. **med** = me.

101. Note the humour of Mercury (incognito) swearing by himself.

104. **ubi,** of time, "when," "as soon as."

105. **ignobilis,** unknown, stranger.

106. **cognosco,** think over.

107. **nimi'**, "very," a meaning frequent in Plautus. Cf. *Pers.* 4. 4. 74 *nimis pauebam*, "I *was* in a fright."

111. **nihil hoc similist similius**, humorously complicated; literally, "nothing is more similar than this similarity."

113. **sane sapio**, "I am in my sound senses" (not *sane* in the meaning of "certainly").

114. **non optempero**, "I don't mind what he says."

115. **si inscendas...poteris**, a not uncommon sequence, though as a general rule *si* takes the same mood in both clauses.

119. **lumbifragium**, "back-breaking," a comic compound not found elsewhere.

124. **uiuo fit...** "In my lifetime I am undergoing what no one will do to me when I am dead." The *imago* was the ancestral image of a distinguished Roman; it was carried in funeral processions. No slave, of course, would ever even possess an *imago*; Sosia speaks humorously.

126. **ille**, intensive, used in appeals to heaven.

127. **pilleus**, a felt skull-cap, worn by slaves after their manumission until their hair (previously shaved) was grown again. The ceremony of receiving the cap took place in the temple of *Feronia*, the goddess of freedmen. Sosia thinks that if Amphitruo does not recognise him as his slave, he will be able to regard himself as a free man.

SCENE II

1. **secundum**, adverb, "behind me."

supsequor (=*subsequor*), "I am following immediately behind." It can be used either with an accusative, as here, or independently.

4. **eccere**, an exclamation, "there!" The origin of this word is a matter of some dispute; it may mean "by Ceres," or "see here in fact" (*ecce re*); or it may be the imperative of an obsolete verb *eccor*, which is a plausible explanation if the common word *ecce* (behold!) is to be derived from the parallel and equally obsolete verb *ecco*.

tuatim, adverb, literally "after your manner." Translate, "just like you."

5. **ut tuis...**, literally, "that to your servants there should be no credence with you." Translate, "it's just like you, not to believe your servants."

7. **scelus**, literally "a crime," here used concretely as a term of reproach, "rascal." Note the jingle with the neighbouring word *scelestam*, "rascally."

9. **sunt.** In Ciceronian Latin we should expect the subjunctive *sint* in this indirect question, but Plautus frequently uses the indicative. Cf. *Capt.* 207 *sentio quam rem agitis.*

14. **in manu,** "in your power."

19. **profecto** (*pro-facto*), an adverb of affirmation, "really," "truly."

20. **tua ex re,** "concerning your business."

21. **ludos facis me,** "mock me." *Ludos-facere* is followed by the accusative *me* because it may be regarded as a single phrase equivalent to *ludificare*; this is common in Plautus.

23. Construe *dicoque ut res facta* (sc. *sit*).

25. **optas.** *Optare* means particularly to wish for a thing difficult of attainment. For the omission of the auxiliary with *facta* cf. preceding note.

27. **quid,** to be taken with the partitive genitive *hominis,* "what sort of a fellow may this be?"

34. **quid est negoti?** "what's the matter?"

41. **sis.** See note on sc. i, l. 25.

44. **ultro,** "to boot."

46. **expetant,** here intransitive ("light upon, fall upon"), a use which is probably only ante-classical.

faxo. Construe *ego faxo* (sc. *ut*) *istaec mendacia in* (*eius*) *tergum expetant.*

48. **ui uerum uincitur,** note the alliteration. "Violence is victorious over veracity."

49. **quo...nam,** to be joined; an instance of tmesis.

puta, "reckon," "consider."

54. "Nor did I at first believe myself—Sosia, until the Sosia there made me believe him."

58. **lact',** i.e. *lacte,* an old form of the nominative *lac.*

59. **dudum** (i.e. *diu-dum,* "it is some time since"), "a little while ago." This is frequent in Plautus, Terence, and the letters and philosophical writings of Cicero; elsewhere it is rare except when coupled with *iam, iamdudum.*

62. "Some mischief has befallen him from an evil hand." In the next line Sosia, mindful of Mercury's flogging, takes this literally.

63. **fateor,** "very true" (literally, "I admit it"). **Pugnis pessume,** note the alliteration.

67. **uno te,** ablative of measure of difference.

70. **offendas,** "find," "meet with." Cf. Cic. *Fam.* II, 3 *imparatum te offendam,* "I will come upon you unawares."

78. Depends on *mirabar,* understood.

83. **blatis,** from *blătio,* "to babble, or prate."

84. **actutum,** "quickly, immediately." The derivation of this word is doubtful: it may mean *uno actu,* i.e. *nulla re intercedente,* the *tum* being enclitic.

85. **exquisito est opus,** "I must enquire into this." *Exquisito,* ablative of the passive participle of *exquiro. Opus,* need, necessity: hence *opus est* (there is need of) is followed by the ablative of the thing needed, really an instrumental ablative. (Occasionally the thing needed is in the nominative.) For this use of the phrase with the passive participle cf. *maturato opus est* ("there is need of haste") in Livy.

88. **sĭmĭtu,** "together" (old form of *simul,* from the same root as *similis.* Gk. ὁμο-, as in ὅμοιος).

89. Construe, *utinam di faxint* (sc. *ut*) *dicta tua re* ("in reality") *infecta eueniant.*

II

The Haunted House

1. Theopropides, on entering the stage, offers thanksgiving to Neptune, the god of the sea, for the end of a very rough and unpleasant voyage.

2. **amisisti,** "let me escape."

3. **pedem latum,** "a foot's breadth," an adverbial accusative of extent, used loosely as the object of *imposisse.*

4. **hau caussast...quin,** "there is no reason why not," i.e. "I give you full permission to do."

imposisse, contracted from *imposiuisse,* =*imposuisse.*

6. **apage,** the Greek imperative ἄπαγε, used as an interjection, "away!" "begone!" It is practically confined to the comic poets.

nunciam, a strengthened form of *iam,* "at this very time."

7. **crediturus fui,** "ever meant to entrust."

8. **edepol.** See note on "A Strange Dilemma," sc. i, l. 1.

10. **Aegypto,** in classical Latin we should expect *ex Aegypto.* Plautus frequently omits the preposition with names of countries: on the other hand, he often uses *ex* or *in* with the names of towns, e.g. *aduenio ex Seleucia* (*Trin.* 4, 2, 3), *in Sicyonem abduxit* (*Pseud.* 4, 6, 36).

11 **exspectatus,** "looked for with eagerness."

12. **exspectatior.** This comparative is ante-classical. Cf. *occlusior,* "more shut," in *Trin.* 1, 2, 185.

14. **interdius,** "in broad daylight." The Romans always kept their house doors open during the day.

19. **factum optume**, literally, "it is most excellently done"; translate, "I am so glad."

20. **quidum**, "why, how?" *Qui* is the old ablative.

22. **seruat**, "is attending to the door."

26. **uah** (alternative form *uaha*), an exclamation of anger (as here), joy or astonishment; Greek, οὐά.

28. **fecisti**, another indirect question in the indicative.

33. **omine**. The bad omen lay in the word *occidisti*; the Romans would consider it unlucky to mention the possibility of anything so inauspicious as murder. Theopropides' imprecation is interrupted by Tranio, and the sentence is unfinished.

34. **istos**. These seem to be the attendants of Theopropides, who had escorted him on his journey.

possies, see note on "A Strange Dilemma," sc. i, l. 57.

37. **attigatis**, ante-classical for *attingatis*.

42. **tutum probe**, "perfectly safe."

44. **capitale**, "atrocious"; really a judicial term, describing crimes which were punishable by death (*caput* in this sense = life).

47. **cĕdo**, an old imperative form, compounded of the particle -*ce* and the root *da*-, meaning "here," "say," and implying great haste or familiarity. Its plural is *cette*, e.g. *Merc.* 5, 4, 4 *cette dextras*, "give me your hands."

48. **hospes necauit hospitem**. The ties of hospitality were held to be peculiarly sacred by the ancient world, and the repetition of the word *hospes* (which in Latin means both "host" and "guest") emphasises, of course here in a mock-heroic style, the iniquity of the murder.

55. **condormiuimus**, the effect of the *con*- is to make the word mean "we fell quite asleep."

56. **oblitus fueram**: another Plautine pluperfect instead of the perfect.

62. **mirum quin**, "he could hardly have."

63. **annis**, "sixty years ago"; in later Latin we should expect *annos*.

67. **Orcus**, the deity who reigned over *Accheruns*, which in Plautus is the name of the land of the dead. Thus "to send a man to Accheruns" means "to kill him," and "to go there oneself" means "to die."

68 **per fidem**, literally "by faith," but intended to be taken in the opposite sense, "by treachery." Thus in Plautus "*Graeca fides*" is proverbial for the ill-faith of the Greeks.

72. **scelestae**, "under a curse."

74. **concrepuit foris**. At this juncture Philolaches and his friends, growing impatient at their enforced silence and in-

activity within the house, try to convey to Tranio outside a hint that it is time the interview is finished.

77. **illisce** (nominative). Tranio is in terror lest their noise should betray the real situation to Theopropides.

79. **apscede ab ianua.** This direction, which is really intended for the unseen Philolaches who is rattling the door, is taken by Theopropides as an address to the supposed ghost in possession of the house.

82. **non me appellabis**, this too is addressed to the obstreperous Philolaches (who has just indiscreetly shouted *heus, Tranio*): the next line is uttered for the benefit of Theopropides, and is meant to propitiate the angry ghost.

84. **quaeso.** Philolaches is not to be repressed, but calls again.

85. **apage hinc te.** Again addressed to those inside, and supposed by the old man to be aimed at the ghost. Tranio's agitation at the disturbance inside the house is most real, though not for the reason which Theopropides thinks.

90. **respexis** =*respexeris* (old future perfect).

92. **scio**, "so you said before."

93. **curassis** =*curaueris* (old future perfect).

94. **quis**, from *queo*, "to be able."

95. **Herculem**, in his character of ἀλεξίκακος, the warder off of evil.

96. **et ego**, the old man would think Tranio meant to add *inuoco*: but the slave, in an aside, finishes the sentence with quite a different turn.

III

The Braggart Captain

1. **clupeus** was the circular iron shield adopted by the Romans from the Etruscans; it was abolished after the Servian reorganisation of the army. It is to be distinguished from the *scutum*, which was four-cornered, made of wood, and covered with leather.

2. **olim** =*illo tempore* in old Latin.

3. **conserta manu**, "when the battle has begun."

4. **praestringat**, "dazzle."

acies, here is a play on two meanings of this word: (1) sight, vision; (2) line of battle. Tyrrell suggests as a translation, "That the foe's array may be dazzled by its rays."

5. **machaera**, Greek μάχαιρα, a sword.

mihi, ethic dative.

7. **quia**, not *quod*, is used by Plautus after verbs of feeling.
feriatam, "idle," participle of *ferior*, to keep holiday, from
feriae.

8. **fartem facere**,"to make mincemeat." Note the alliteration.
Fartem from *farcio*, to stuff.

9. **ubi hic**, "whereabout here."

Artotrogus, from the Greek ἄρτος and τρώγω, "Bread-
gnawer," an appropriate name for a parasite.

uirum, refers, of course, to Pyrgopolinices himself.

12. **ad**, "in comparison with," like the Greek παρά, πρός.
The phrase must not be taken too closely with *aequiperare*,
which is always followed by the dative or by *cum* with the
ablative: cf. *aequiperata cum fratre gloria* in Cic. *Mur.* 14, 31.

13. **Curculioneis**, a word comically coined; perhaps here,
as in *Trin.* 4, 3, 11, there is a play on its similarity to the
word *currere*, "in the plains of the Runaways."

14. **Clutomestoridysarchides**, from the Greek κλυτός, μήστωρ,
and δύσαρχία. Both words are comically formed, for the sake
of their sound, like *Therapontigonus Platagidorus* in another of
Plautus' plays, the *Curculio*. Translate, "Bombastes Furioso."

16. **cum** in Plautus often couples subject and attribute
where later Latin would have an adjective or participle, cf.
l. 658 of this play, *homines cum istis moribus*.

18. **pāniculus**, "reed": except in Plautus, it is feminine,
pānicula. Examples of similar variations in gender are *guttur*
and *dorsus* (masculine in Plautus and neuter in later Latin),
praesepis (feminine in Plautus and neuter, *praesepe*, later).

20. **quae tu...**, an aside, not intended to be heard by
Pyrgopolinices.

21. **peiiuriorem**, "more of a liar."

hoc...quam illic (next line). Note the strengthened form of
comparison, which occurs also in Cicero.

22. **gloriarum**, "doughty deeds." The plural *gloriae* means
in classical Latin: (1) glory achieved in several cases, e.g.
ueteres Gallorum gloriae in Tac. *An.* III, 45; (2) boasts.

24. **nisi unum**, "the only thing is this."

epityrum, "olive-salad," eaten by the Romans with cheese.
estur =*editur*. **insanum**, used as an adverb, a piece of slang,
"most awfully." Cf. *Bacch.* 4, 51 *insanum magnum molior
negotium*.

25. **eccum**, sc. *me*, "here I am." In conversational language
ecce is combined with certain forms of *is*, *ille* and *iste*, into one
word, with a demonstrative force.

uel, "for instance."

26. **bracchium**; the parasite purposely says "arm" instead of "thigh," in order to raise a laugh.

28. **at indiligenter iceram**, "I was but playing."

30. **transmineret** occurs nowhere else but here; it is formed like *eminere, imminere*.

34. **dentiant**, "grow" (of teeth). Note the pun with *dentes*. "Lest our *tooth* have *too thin* a fare."

41. **praeolat**, "perceive beforehand."

43. **Scytholatronia**, formed from *Scythes* (Scythians) and *latrones* (mercenaries).

44. **Sardeis**, an archaic form of the nominative plural of the 2nd declension, and equivalent to *Sardi*, "natives of Sardes." Cf. l. 374 of this play, *non possunt mihi minis tuis hisce oculis exfodiri*, "my eyes cannot be dug out by threats from you" (for *hisce* as nominative cf. *illisce* in "The Haunted House," l. 77).

49. **offae**. *Offa* = a bit, or mouthful. Hence in Latin *inter os atque offam* (quoted by Cato) means "'twixt the cup and the lip."

51. **communicabo**, "I will share." The usual construction of this verb is *communicare aliquid cum aliquo*.

53. **foret** = *fuisset*.

54. **peditastelli**, a diminutive of *peditaster*, which, however, is never found to be used in Latin. The ending *-aster* is depreciatory, as in the word *parasitaster* (in Terence), from *parasitus*; and the further diminutive form *-ellus* expresses still more contempt. Translate, "wretched foot-soldiers."

56. **Pyrgopolinicem**, literally, "Tower-town-taker."

unum. *Unus* is often used in Plautus to strengthen superlatives, e.g. *tu, quam ego unam uidi mulierem audacissumam* (*Asin.* 521), "the very boldest woman I have seen."

IV

The Shipwreck

SCENE I

1. **Palaemo**, a Greek sea-deity. The Roman equivalent was *Portunus*.

2. **Herculei**, an old form of the genitive *Herculi*, the most usual genitive being *Herculis*. Hercules was the god of those who travel by land and by water.

3. **mulierculas**, diminutive of *mulieres*, used here to denote not so much the smallness of the heroines, as their frailness and inability to buffet the waves.

5. **eugae,** Greek εὖγε, an exclamation of joy and admiration, "bravo," "well done."

perbene, note the *per-*, meaning "very."

7. **potuit,** sc. *auortere*.

9. **deuitauerint,** "if once they escape." The future perfect is demanded by the sense.

11. **eugepae,** contracted from *euge papae*, the latter word being from the Greek παπαί, "wonderful!"

12. **foras,** an accusative form like *alias*, from an obsolete nominative *fora*, of which *foris* is an ablative form; "out," "forth."

13. **se capessit,** "betakes herself."

14. **autem,** "in turn."

17. **in malam crucem,** "to destruction." This phrase is frequently used as an imprecation.

18. **hem,** expressing pity.

hodie, "this blessed day," expressing not so much time-when, as the excitement of the speaker.

20. **compendium facere,** "to make short work of." Cf. *compendium ego te facere pultandi uolo* (*Pseud.* 2, 2, 11), "I should like you to save your knocking," i.e. "stop knocking."

21. **uesperi,** "at their expense," literally, "from their evening meal." Cf. *M.G.* 4, 2, 5 *de uesperi suo uiuere*, "to live on his own supper," i.e. "to be his own master."

Scene II

1. **nimio** =*multo*; to be joined with *minus miserae*.

memorantur, "are recounted," i.e. in speech.

2. **quam in usu,** "than in actual fact."

experiundo..., literally, "bitterness is added to them (i.e. *fortunis*) by experience." Translate actively.

3. **deo complacitumst,** "heaven has decreed."

5. **rem,** "disaster." **memorabo,** future indicative denoting deliberation. "Am I to say?"

6. **partem,** "lot."

7. **labori,** predicative dative.

potiri, in Latin takes either (1) the accusative (as here), or (2) the ablative, e.g. *Pseud.* 1071 *ille si illa sit potitus muliere*, "if he has won that woman," or (3) the genitive, when it is equivalent to *particeps fieri*, e.g. *regni potiri*, "to gain a share in the kingdom," Cic. *Fam.* 1, 7, 5.

9. **id,** i.e. *me impiare*.

curaui ut cauerem, "I have tried to avoid."

10. **indecore, inique, inmodeste.** Note the asyndeton, which is

expressive of Palaestra's indignation at the gods' unfair treatment of her. Cf. l. 33 of this scene, and l. 41 of the next, where asyndeton is used to emphasise the pathos of the situation.

12. **si ad hunc...**, literally, "if in this way there is among you reward for the guiltless," i.e. "if this is the way you reward the guiltless."

13. **sciam**, for *scirem*; a rejected condition of present time. Construe, *si scirem me aut parentes sceleste fecisse.*

15. **erile scelus**, "the crime of my master" (*erus*), i.e. Labrax, to whom, in the play, Palaestra was bound as a slave, and with whom she was voyaging when the shipwreck occurred.

eiius, as though *eri scelus* had preceded.

male habet, "distresses."

17. **quae simul uecta mecum est**, "my fellow-passenger," i.e. Ampelisca.

19. **quae**, i.e. Ampelisca, who certainly was not mentioned in the last sentence, but Palaestra's agitated frame of mind must be held responsible for her somewhat incoherent lamentations.

21. **consili**, partitive genitive dependent on *quid*.

22. **sola solis**, note emphasis, and cf. "The Haunted House," l. 48, and note.

24. **obuiam** (literally, *ob-uiam*, "in the way"), "to meet," with verbs of motion.

25. **quod**, depends on *induta*, accusative like that after a Greek middle voice.

oppido (etymology doubtful; possibly connected with the Greek ἔμπεδον), "absolutely."

26. **quo sim**, dependent deliberative question, "nor do I know how to get food or where to get shelter."

31. **an**, note the omission of *utrum*.

incerta, followed by *consili*. It is thus used with the genitive by Livy and Tacitus, but never by Cicero. Perhaps most commonly it is followed by a relative clause, e.g. *cum incertus essem, ubi esses.* Cic. *Att.* 1, 9, 1.

32. **conspicor**, "to perceive," a word frequent only in Plautus and Caesar.

33. **algor, error, pauor**, see note on l. 10.

34. **haec**, "these things," i.e. the sentence *me ita miseram esse.*

36. **leibera** = *libera.*

prognata fui = *prognata sum*. This form of the perfect passive is frequent in Plautus. Cf. *Most.* 695 *non mihi uisum fuit:* and "The Miser," sc. ii, l. 54.

maxume, "as much as any."

37. **qui**, old ablative, "in what way am I now less a slave...?"

Scene III

1. **in rem,** "advantageous." **secludam,** "banish."

2. **exanimalis** can be either active, "killing" (as here) or passive, "lifeless," e.g. *ni illum exanimalem faxo*, "unless I kill him," *Bacch.* 4, 8, 7.

3. **uitae hau parco,** "I care not for my life."

4. **latebris,** local ablative with *perreptaui*.

5. **quaerere,** an infinitive of purpose (Plautine), dependent on *perreptaui*. Cf. *Trin.* 4, 3, 8 *recurre petere*, "run back to find."

6. **neque consultumst,** sc. *mihi*, "nor have I decided."

9. **uiua** = *dum uiuo*.

10. **quoianam.** *Quoia* is an archaic form of *cuius* (cf. "A Strange Dilemma," sc. i, l. 11), an interrogative pronoun found most frequently in Plautus and Terence: though cf. Verg. *Ecl.* iii, 1 *cuium pecus? an Meliboei?* "whose flock? Does it belong to Meliboeus?"

14. **subuenta,** imperative of *subuento*, frequentative of *subuenio*, "come and help."

15. **eximes,** "will you deliver?"; used with either *ex* (as here) or *de* or the simple ablative. **miseram,** sc. *me*.

16. **tetigit,** "fell upon."

18. **opsecro,** a polite expression of entreaty, practically equivalent to an interjection, "Pray," "I beseech you."

20. **hem,** "dear me."

23. **mihi es aemula,** "your desire is mine."

24. **gradu,** "step by step."

26. **cedo,** see note on "The Haunted House," l. 47.

30. **leuas,** "lighten, relieve"; like many verbs in old Latin, this takes the genitive as well as the ablative.

31. **praeloqui,** *prae*, "in advance," has the same sense as *occupas*. Cf. the Greek φθάνω.

32. **amabo,** "pray," an expression used by women.

34. **grassabimur,** "shall we go?" Chiefly ante-classical, and never in Cicero or Caesar.

38. **decorum,** used with the ablative like *dignum*. Cf. *M.G.* 619 *facinora neque te decora neque tuis uirtutibus*, "deeds worthy neither of you nor of your prowess."

40. **quisquis est deus,** a common formula where the name of the deity is unknown, as he might be angered by a specific wrong conjecture.

SCENE IV

1. **preces**, "boons"; *prex* is properly "a thing asked"; "a mode of asking" is a further development of its meaning.

2. **precantum** =*precantium*; dependent on *uox*.

3. **bonam**, "kind"; **grauatam**, "grudging," from *grauor*.

4. **exsequontur**, "seek."

8. **maestiter**, adverb of *maestus*, occurs only here.

9. **imus**, "we have been walking."

longule, "rather far," diminutive of *longe*, found elsewhere in Plautus.

11. **caerulas**, a by-form of *caeruleas*. "The blue highways" means, of course, the sea.

12. **aequius erat**, "it would have been more befitting," followed by the accusative and infinitive—*uos uenire*.

13. **candidatas**, "clothed in white," used in this sense only in Plautus and in post-Augustan prose. It later acquired its meaning of "candidate for office" because Roman candidates wore a "glittering white" toga.

hostiatas (from *hostia*, a sacrificial victim), "provided with victims."

14. **ueniri solet**, note the passive construction, and translate "it is not the custom for people to come."

15. **quae...simus**, "seeing that."

18. **nesciis**. *Nescius* (*ne-scio*) has two meanings: (1) active (very common), "ignorant, unaware"; (2) passive (as here, but very rare), "not known, strange." Cf. *Capt.* 265 *siquid nescibo, id nescium tradam tibi*, "whatever I do not know, I shall give you for unknown." *Ignotus, notus, gnarus*, and *dubius* also are found in both active and passive senses.

21. **parata**, "at hand."

24. **me**, ablative of comparison. **feminarum**, genitive after *nulla*, "no woman."

26. **colo**, "support."

28. **fateor**, "yes."

clueo. This verb existed in old Latin (like the Greek κλύω) in the special sense of "to be spoken of." Cf. *Trin.* 2, 2, 28 *uictor uictorum cluet*, "he is called conqueror of conquerors."

29. **quidquid est**, "everything."

32. **nostrum**, objective genitive of the personal pronoun, for *nostri* (which is not found in Plautus) or *nobis*.

V

The Twins

SCENE I

1. illanc = *illam*, i.e. the wife of Menaechmus I. Frightened by the pretended madness of Menaechmus II, she has gone in search of a doctor.

amoui, "I have got rid of."

inpurissumum, "most objectionable person."

2. imperas. Here, as in *iubes* (l. 5), Menaechmus addresses Apollo, who, he pretends, is sending a fit of madness upon him. The wildness of his ensuing conversation is explained by this pretence.

Note the cumulative effect of *membra atque ossa atque artua*, which mean practically the same thing, but, put thus, add emphasis to Menaechmus' threat.

artua, an alternative (neuter) form of the ordinary plural *artus* ("limbs"). It seems to occur only here in extant Latin, but is quoted by the grammarian Nonius from this passage.

3. dabitur malum, "it will go ill with you." The old man, though nearly paralysed with fright, tries to bluster and appear undismayed.

6. "I will cudgel him to the bone."

assulatim, "in splinters," "piecemeal," from *assula* (diminutive of *axis*), "a splinter."

7. enim uero, "of a truth, to be sure." Unlike *enim*, this phrase usually begins a sentence.

8. ut, causal.

11. proteram, "crush, destroy."

edentulus, "toothless" (*e-dens*).

14. pedum pernicitas, "swiftness of their feet," must be regarded as *pedes pernices* in order to be taken with *inflexa*, which must obviously be applied to something concrete, not abstract. This high-sounding incoherency may be attributed to the inspiration of Apollo.

18. demutat, "changes, violates." This word does not occur in the Ciceronian period.

19. eu, Greek εὖ.

hercle, contracted from *Hercule*, the vocative of *Hercules*: sometimes with the prefix *me—mehercle*. A popular oath or asseveration.

morbum, exclamatory accusative. "What a severe and obstinate disease."

·

20. **uel**, intensive particle, "even."

quam ualuit, "how well he was."

22. **eibo** = *ibo*.

accersam. *Accerso* is a by-form of *arcesso*, and is used more often by Sallust than by other writers.

iam quantum potest, to be taken together, "as quickly as possible." The old man now goes off for the doctor, and Menaechmus is left alone.

23. **quaeso**, literally, "I entreat," hence "pray," "prithee," often thrown into a sentence parenthetically, as an intensive expression.

24. **ualidus**, emphatic, "although I am perfectly well."

25. **saluo**, sc. *mihi*, dependent on *licet*, "while I may in safety."

26. **uosque**. Here he turns to the audience, and admonishes them, as Plautine characters occasionally do.

27. **ni** was originally identical with *ne*, and spelt *nei*; it was quite a simple negative, as it appears in the phrases *quidni, nimirum* ("not wonderful"). Its use (exemplified here) in imperative clauses, like *ne*, is ante-classical and poetical. Later, of course, it = *nisi*.

me, object of *indicetis*. Omit in translation.

29. **medicum**, object of the gerund *manendo*. Cf. Lucretius, I, 111 *Aeternas poenas in morte timendumst* (equivalent to *poenae timendae sunt*).

31. **obligasse**, in its literal (and quite classical) meaning of "to bind up, bandage." Its meaning "to put under an obligation" is a later development.

Aesculapio, Apollini, datives of interest.

34. **formicinum**, "crawling," literally "like ants" (*formica*).

SCENE II

1. **morbi**, partitive genitive dependent on *quid*.

2. **laruatus**, "bewitched," from *larua*, a ghost, really the soul of a dead man who had come to an unjust or untimely end. These *laruae* were supposed usually to take the form of skeletons or spectres, and to strike the living with madness.

cerritus, "crazed," contracted from *cerebritus*, from *cerebrum*, the brain.

3. **ueternus**, from *uetus* ("old"), primarily "old age," hence (as here) "lethargy," as the disease of old people.

intercus, from *inter* and *cutis*, "under the skin"; hence as an adjective with *aqua* = dropsy.

4. The old man resents the doctor asking the questions which he has been summoned to answer.

5. **perfacile**; note the significance of the *per*. The doctor's extraordinary mixture of complacency and cowardice is exceedingly well drawn.

10. **hominem.** Menaechmus I, arriving by chance, is subjected to the professional diagnosis which is intended for his brother.

11. **ne**, an interjection, Greek ναί, "truly, verily." Cf. *Amph.* I, I, 169 *ne ego homo infelix fui*, and "The Miser," sc. ii, l. 44.

peruorsus, literally, "turned the wrong way," i.e. "awry."

aduorsus, literally, "set opposite, in hostile opposition to," i.e. "unfavourable."

12. **fecit palam**, "proclaimed abroad." Cf. Nepos, *Han.* 7, 7 *hac re palam facta*, "when this matter had been announced."

14. **Ulixes**, Ulysses, famous for his craft.

regi, literally, "king," hence "patron," often used in this sense. Cf. *Capt.* 92 *meus est rex potitus hostium*, "my patron has fallen into the hands of the enemy."

15. **hominem uita euoluam sua**, "I will strip him of his life," i.e. "slay him."

16. Menaechmus decides that it is foolish to talk about the parasite's life, because, as the parasite lived entirely at Menaechmus' expense, everything that belonged to the parasite —even his life—belonged ultimately to Menaechmus.

19. **saluos sis**, "how do you do?"

apertas (frequentative of *aperio*), "lay bare."

20. **isti**, "that disease you know about, that we have already discussed." Really, of course, it was the other brother who had discussed it.

21. **quin tu te suspendis?** "Go and hang yourself": the interrogative is dropped in English.

quidni (cf. note on sc. i, l. 27), "why not?" It introduces a rhetorical question (contrast *cur non*, which always expects an answer) and is followed by the subjunctive.

22. **ellebori**, "hellebore," a plant much used by the ancients as a remedy for mental diseases. Cf. *Pseud.* 1185 *elleborum hisce hominibus opus est*, "these men want a dose of hellebore."

iungere, ablative of an otherwise unknown noun *iungus*; translate, "by the aid of."

24. **in malam crucem**, see note on "The Shipwreck," sc. i, l. 17. The doctor is trying to ask leading questions which shall help him in his diagnosis; Menaechmus, unconscious of any

need for a diagnosis at all, regards the questions as impertinent and absurd.

25. **primulum**; note the diminutive; "he is just beginning a little to...."

26. **esse**, contracted infinitive of *edere*, "to eat." Other contracted forms of this verb, *es, est, estis*, etc., are not to be confused with parts of *esse*, "to be."

32. **locusta**, "lobster."

34. **perdormiscin**, "do you sleep *on*?"; note the force of the *per-*.

cubans, "when you are in bed."

36. **qui**, old ablative of manner; "in which case."

38. **Nestor**, famous among the heroes before Troy for his wisdom. "A perfect Solomon of wisdom."

de uerbis, "in the matter of speech."

praeut, see note on "A Strange Dilemma," sc. i, l. 39.

39. **rabiosam canem**, "a mad dog." This insult had, in fact, been offered to the wife by Menaechmus I; Menaechmus II is naturally bewildered by such an incriminating suggestion.

42. **haec ted arguo**, "I charge you with this." *Arguo* can be thus followed by a double accusative, cf. Lucr. VI, 405 *quid undas arguit?* "Of what does he impeach the waves?" The cause of complaint is generally put in the genitive, e.g. *aliquem facinoris arguere*, "to accuse some one of a crime."

43. "I know that you stole the sacred garland from the head of Jupiter," an unspeakable act of sacrilege. Note these four lines all ending in *scio*, to emphasise Menaechmus' wrath.

45. **furca**, "yoke," an instrument of punishment in the form of a fork, which was placed on the culprit's neck, while his hands were fastened at the two ends. Hence the word *furcifer*, "a yoke-bearer," is a common term of abuse, "hang-dog."

49. **non** = *nonne?*

scin quid facias optumum est? A loose construction, equivalent to *scisne quid optumum sit (ut) facias?* **est**, Plautus frequently uses the indicative in indirect questions.

50. **quippini**, "why not?" Cf. note on *ni*, sc. i, l. 27.

55. **proinde ut...**, "in view of what I see of his insanity."

56. **immo**, "nay, rather." Neither doctor nor father-in-law is in the least anxious to be left alone with the madman.

57. **parentur**, sc. *ea*, "those things," antecedent to *quibus*.

quibu' paratis, "the preparation of which."

59. **pro**, see note on "A Strange Dilemma," sc. i, l. 41.

62. **coepio**, "begin." This present form occurs only in ante-classical Latin. In later times the perfect form *coepi* has a present meaning, and its object is usually an infinitive (active more often than passive) rather than a noun (as *pugnas* here) or pronoun.

64. **perperam**, "wrongly," an adverb taking the form of the accusative feminine of *perperus*, which is only ante- and post-classical, and is derived from the Greek πέρπερος, "vainglorious." For the adverb taking the accusative form cf. *foras*, "The Shipwreck," sc. i, l. 12.

ipsi insaniunt; really concessive, but loosely tacked on.

66. **huc**, the house next door to his own. The background to the Roman stage always represented two adjoining houses.

VI

The Miser

Scene I

1. **age**, "come, come on."

2. **circumspectatrix**, literally, "she who spies around," i.e. "spy," "pry-about."

emissiciis, literally "sent forth," hence, by a picturesque turn of meaning, "inquisitive." Plautus has a similarly formed word in *Poen.* 5, 5, 24 *demissiciae*, "hanging down," i.e. "long, flowing," applied to *tunicae* (tunics).

3. **nam qur** = *curnam*. Plautus frequently changes the order of this compound. Cf. l. 5 *nam qua* = *quanam*.

ut misera sis, "to give you some reason to call yourself wretched."

4. Construe, *ut aetatem-malam dignam te-mala exigas*.

aetas is, in the comic poets, often equivalent to *uita*.

6. **stimulorum seges**, "harvest of whips," a picturesque form of abuse. Cf. Verg. *Aen.* III, 46 *telorum seges*, "a crop of weapons."

7. **sis**, see note on "A Strange Dilemma," sc. i, l. 25.

8. **incedit**, "she creeps," always used of slow movement. Cf. Verg. *Aen.* I, 46 *ego quae diuum incedo regina*, "I who walk majestically as the queen of the gods."

10. **testudineum gradum**, "tortoise-pace"; cf. *formicinus gradus* in "The Twins," sc. i, l. 34.

11. **diui** =*di*. This is the only place in Plautus in which this nominative occurs.

adaxint =*adegerint. Axim* (=*egerim*) is formed in the same way as *faxim* (cf. *faxo*, "A Strange Dilemma," sc. i, l. 20).

ad suspendium, "to the gallows."

13. **scelesta sola secum,** note the alliteration, cf. ll. 10, 22, 27.

15. **rerum,** dependent on *quid,* "what of things," i.e. "what."

18. **digitum transuorsum,** "a finger's breadth"; a common phrase, found also in Cato.

19. **respexis** =*respexeris* (contracted, the original form having been *respexesis*).

donicum, "until," ante- and post-classical form of *donec;* formed from the old dative *doni,* i.e. *dioni* (from the same root as *dies*) and the conjunction *cum;* literally, "at the time of day when."

20. **te dedam...,** i.e. "the cross shall teach you to keep your eyes shut for ever." "I'll send you for a schooling to the gallows" (Thornton).

21. **scelestiorem....** From here to the end of his speech Euclio soliloquises in an aside; he then goes back into his house.

23. **duit,** an archaic subjunctive present of *dare;* cf. note on *sim,* "A Strange Dilemma," sc. i, l. 57.

uerba dare, "to give mere words instead of deeds," i.e. "to deceive."

inprudenti, "unaware, unexpecting" (lit. *in-pro-uidens*).

24. **persentiscat,** intensive form of *persentio.* "Smell out the place where the gold is hidden."

25. **occipitium,** from *ob, caput,* "the back part of the head."

26. **estne,** a loose construction, in sense an indirect question after *uisam.*

28. **noenum,** an old collateral form of *non,* contracted from *ne-oenum,* i.e. *nec-unum* (like *nihil* from *ne-hilum,* "not anything"). Cf. the famous line of Ennius, *Noenum rumores ponebat ante salutem,* "he did not value vague rumours above certain safety." *Noenum* here goes with *queo,* two lines below.

30. **comminisci,** "to devise."

32. **nescio quae,** "some." **intemperiae,** "whims."

33. **peruigilat.** For the force of the *per-* cf. *perdormiscin* in the previous extract, sc. ii, l. 34.

interdius, see "The Haunted House," l. 14.

34. **claudus sutor,** "a lame cobbler."

35. Re-enter Euclio, having satisfied himself that his treasure is safe.

defaecato (from *de* and *faex*), literally, "to cleanse from dregs," hence "to make clear, set at ease." For the primary meaning cf. *uindemiae defaecatae*, "wines on the lees well refined" in Isaiah xxv, 6; and for the metaphorical sense in this passage cf. the phrase *liquido animo* in *Pseud.* 232.

39. **quaesti**, archaic genitive of *quaestus*; depends on *nihil aliud*. Other nouns, too, such as *senatus*, *tumultus* were in early Latin declined according to the 2nd *and* the 4th declension.

40. **inaniis oppletae**, "filled with emptiness," oxymoron.

41. **mirum quin faciat**, "I wonder he does not make me." Philippus and Darius are mentioned as the best known examples of wealthy kings, the one as a European, the other as an Asiatic monarch.

42. **triuenefica** (*ter-uenenum-facio*), "an arrant poison-mixer," i.e. "sorceress, hag."

45. **iam ego hic ero**, "I shall soon be back again."

47. **quod**, "if," properly "as regards the case that." In this sense it is always followed by the subjunctive.

49. **uiuet**, picturesquely spoken of the fire. Readers of Dickens will remember "The Old Curiosity Shop," chap. 44, "The fire has been alive as long as I have."

extempulo, "immediately"; this is the original uncontracted form of *extemplo*.

52. **utenda rogant**, "borrow." Similarly, *utenda dare* means "to lend."

56. **Bona Fortuna**, "Good Luck herself." The miser's wariness is carried to excess.

58. **nusquam quaquam**, a very strong negation; "nowhere at all."

60. **pessulus**, "a bolt"; ante- and post-classical.

61. **animi**, a locative-genitive dependent on *discrucior*.

63. **magister curiae**, "president of the curia." The *curia* was one of the thirty parts into which Romulus was said to have divided the Roman people. It is, however, probable that this phrase was intended by Plautus as a translation (see introduction) of the Greek τριττυάρχης, for distributions such as Euclio here describes were common at Athens, but were practically unknown at Rome before the time of the Emperors.

64. **diuidere**, a loose construction for *se diuisurum esse*. Nummos, in a general sense "coins, money"; it only rarely in Plautus refers to the *sestertius*.

65. **ilico** (=*in loco*), literally "on the spot, there," hence, "immediately."

67. **ueri simile**, "probable."

68. **pauxillum**, diminutive of *paucus*, and mostly ante-

classical. To be taken here closely with *parui*, which is a genitive of price or value dependent on *facere*.

70. **benignius salutant**, "they are more profuse in their compliments." The original sense of the word *benignus* (i.e. *benigenus*, from *bonus-genus*) is "generous, profuse," rather than "kind," as our English word tends to suggest.

72. **copulantur dextras**, "shake hands." This is the only passage in which this verb is deponent.

74. **profectus sum**, "where I've set out to go."

75. **rusum quantum...**, "I shall come back again as quickly as possible."

SCENE II

Congrio is the name of the cook, who has been sent by Megadorus, the prospective bridegroom of Euclio's daughter, to supervise the preparation of the wedding-supper.

1. **attatae**, Greek ἀτταταί, an exclamation of joy, pain, astonishment, or warning.

incola, "one who dwells in a place," "inhabitant."

accola, "one who dwells near a place," "neighbour."

aduena, "one who comes to a place," "stranger."

3. **Bacchae**, "furious women," from the Greek βάκχαι, women raving under the inspiration of the god Bacchus. In the time of Plautus, the worship of this god was carried on in Italy with the wildest and most outrageous forms of celebration, and was prohibited by a famous decree of the Senate in 186 B.C. It is doubtful, however, whether this line contains a reference to the historical episode.

bacchanal, a place where the festivals of Bacchus were celebrated.

4. **discipuli**, i.e. the inferior cooks of whom Congrio was in charge.

5. **oppido** (adverb), colloquial, "completely, very much."

gymnasium, Greek γυμνάσιον, a school for gymnastic exercises; here used comically, "the old man has been exercising his muscles on me," i.e. flogging me.

9. **ipsu'**, see note on "A Strange Dilemma," sc. i, l. 80.

magister, i.e. Euclio.

10. **ligna**, literally "wood," a play on words. Wood was of course a necessity to the cooks, in order to light the fire; Euclio had produced a plentiful supply of wooden cudgels.

usquam gentium, "anywhere in the world."

11. **onustos fustibus**, "laden with cudgels"; translate, "illustrated with cuts."

Before Congrio can escape the onslaughts of the suspicious miser, the latter comes out in pursuit.

12. **tene, tene,** "stop him, stop him."

13. **tresuiros.** The *tresuiri* were the Roman magistrates who had charge of the prisons, and punished those whom they found trespassing against the security of the public. Cf. the reflection of Sosia in *Amph.* I, I, 3 *quid faciam nunc, si tresuiri me in carcerem compegerint?*

defero nomen, "to enter a name," i.e. to impeach or accuse someone before a magistrate (a common technical term).

15. **istuc.** Congrio considers himself to blame, not for having threatened Euclio in self-defence, but for having neglected the opportunity of stabbing him.

16. **uiuat.** *uiuere* is frequently used by Plautus as the equivalent of *esse.* Cf. *Trin.* 390 lepidus *uiuis,* "you're a jolly man."

19. **mollior magi'.** In colloquial language the Romans frequently strengthened comparatives by adding *magis.* Cf. *Stich.* 698 *hoc magis est dulcius,* "this is sweeter."

cinaedus, "dancer."

20. **nos,** direct object after the verbal noun *tactio,* in English "the touching (of) us." A striking parallel instance of this usage occurs *A sin.* 920 *quid tibi huc receptio ad test meum uirum?* "What business have you to receive my husband here at your house?" where *huc, ad te,* and *meum uirum* all depend on the noun *receptio.* This construction is comparable with that of the gerund when subject to *est.*

quae res? An expression of indignation. "What's that?"

22. **sine,** "very well, granted": properly the imperative of *sino,* but here, as elsewhere, practically an interjection.

caput, from its importance in the anatomical system, is practically equivalent to *ego.*

23. **fuat,** archaic present subjunctive of *sum,* used often by Plautus, but only once by Terence.

24. **quid** to be joined with *nam,* and followed by the partitive genitive *negoti.*

26. **coctum,** supine, "we came to cook."

malum, imprecation, "plague take you."

27. **edim,** subjunctive. See note on "A Strange Dilemma," sc. i, l. 57.

tutor, "guardian," always of persons, e.g. of minors or lunatics; contrast *curator,* which means "guardian of an estate." Translate, "you aren't my keeper, are you?"

29. Note the emphasis of *meae, mea.*

31. **me hau paenitet**, "I have nothing to grumble about," "I am content enough."

tua ne expetam, a concise expression, equivalent to *ne existumes me tua expetere*, "don't suppose I want *your* property." (*Me* and *tua* first in their respective clauses, to emphasise the contrast.)

32. **quid est qua prohibes gratia**, "what reason have you for forbidding...."

33. **secu' quam uelles**, "otherwise than as you wish," i.e. "against your wishes."

35. **peruium**, "a thoroughfare, passage"; to be taken closely with facitis as forming with it a transitive verb, "do the round of."

36. **focum**, the hiding-place of the pot of gold.

37. **fissile caput**, "a broken head." *Fissilis* is a very rare adjective, derived from *findo*, "to cleave."

39. **nisi iussero**, "against my orders."

41. Euclio departs into the house.

42. **Lauerna**, originally the goddess of darkness, and hence, naturally, the patroness of thieves. Congrio's appeal to her suggests that Euclio's suspicions of his character are not ill founded.

43. **pipulo**, "with an outcry": a very rare word.

differam, "confound, distract." In this sense it is more usually found in the passive, e.g. *Epid.* 1, 2, 15 *differor clamore*, "I am disquieted by a shout." This meaning is exclusively ante-classical.

44. **ne**, see note on sc. ii, l. 11, of the last extract.

auspicio malo, "under unfavourable auspices." Any references to *auspicia* have, of course, a peculiarly Roman colour.

45. **nummo**, ablative of price. "I was hired for money."

mercede, doubly in the ablative, denoting both comparison and "what there is need of." Note the alliteration and general assonance with *medico*; perhaps "a stretcher more than a stiver."

46. **hoc**, i.e. the money, which Euclio now brings out with him, unable to rest while it remains in the house subject to the investigations of untrustworthy cooks.

48. **tibicinae**, "flute-players," who always took part in Roman wedding-celebrations.

49. **gregem uenalium**, "gang of slaves."

51. **temperi**, "and about time too": really the locative case of *tempus*, "early."

fissorum, from *fissum* (really the passive participle of *findo*), "holes."

52. **opera huc...,** "I hired you to work, not to talk."

54. **conductus fui** =*conductus sum*; cf. note on "The Shipwreck," sc. ii, l. 36.

55. **lege agito mecum,** "go to law against me," if you want to argue further; in the meantime, **molestus ne sis,** "don't be a nuisance."

56. **in malum cruciatum** =*in malam crucem*.

abi tu modo, "go yourself." Here Congrio returns to the house, leaving Euclio alone on the stage.

58. **pauper,** i.e. himself (Euclio). **Opulento homine,** i.e. Megadorus, his prospective son-in-law.

rem habere, "to have dealings."

59. **Megadorus, miserum modis,** note the alliteration here and in the four following lines.

62. **condigne,** "very worthily." This word nearly always gives its sentence a sarcastic or ironical turn.

gallus gallinacius, "the poultry cock."

63. **peculiaris,** "belonging especially to," "the peculiar property of"; derived, like the word *peculium* ("property") and *pecunia* from *pecus* ("cattle"), because in the earliest times property consisted of cattle.

paenissume (superlative of *paene*), "very nearly."

64. **scalpurrire** (from *scalpo*), "to scratch"; occurs only in this passage.

65. **circumcirca,** "all around," a strengthened *circum* or *circa*; very rare.

peracuit, "became exasperated." Cf. *Bacch.* 1099 *hoc est quo pectus peracescit,* "this is the cause of the fury in my breast."

67. **mercedem si id...,** "a reward for revealing the gold." The gold being the matter always uppermost in Euclio's mind, *id*, to him, requires no explanation.

68. **manubrium,** properly "a hilt, handle"; hence used figuratively to mean "an occasion, opportunity."

VII

The Parasite

2. **turbauerint,** "have created a disturbance." In this sense *turbo* in Latin approaches slang.

quippiam, "in any way." (Neuter accusative.)

4. **aegre est mi,** "it grieves me." Note the colloquial use of the adverb with *sum*, and cf. the common phrase *frustra esse,* "to be mistaken."

hunc, i.e. Hegio.

facere quaestum carcerarium, literally, "to carry on the trade of keeping a prison," i.e. "to turn gaoler."

5. **gnati.** Hegio has in his possession certain enemy captives, whom he is anxious to exchange for his own son.

6. **ille,** the son, Philopolemus.

conciliari = (in old Latin) "to be bought, obtained." *Concilio* is literally "to call together" (*con* =*cum*, and *-cil-* is from the root *cal* which appears in the Greek καλέω). Cf. *concilium.*

7. **carnuficina** = the office of executioner; hence *carnuficinam facere* =*carnificem esse.*

possum perpeti, literally, "I can endure...." Translate independently of the rest of the sentence, "I shouldn't mind."

8. **maerore maceror.** Note the alliteration here, and in the next line the assonance of the three verbs ending in *-esco.*

9. **consenesco,** "waste away" (literally "with old age").

10. **misera.** We naturally expect the line to end with some word denoting sorrow. Plautus gives it a humorous turn by the unexpected but obvious "leanness."

11. **quod edo domi,** "what I eat at home." As a matter of fact Ergasilus is too poor to have any food at home. Hence his great anxiety to procure an invitation to a meal elsewhere.

12. **aliquantillum.** Note the diminutive, "the tiniest taste elsewhere."

beat, "does me good."

14. **ne fle.** The imperative with *ne*, in prohibitions, is used only in the poets. Cf. Vergil, *tu ne cede malis*, "do not give in to misfortune."

16. **intellexi,** sc. *esse amicum.*

17. **tum denique,** emphatic from its position, and pointing forward to *quom*, "only when we have lost the blessings we had."

19. **potitust hostium,** "has fallen into the hands of the enemy." *Potior*, like most Latin deponents, is really a middle rather than a passive form. *Potior alicuius* ="I put myself in possession of something."

20. **quanti fuerit,** "how dear he was." Genitive of price or value.

21. **incommodum,** neuter form of the adjective used as a noun, "misfortune, injury"; a classical use.

24. **dixis** =*dixeris*, **induxis** =*induxeris. Animum inducere* = "to suppose, imagine"; an alternative form is *in animum inducere.*

26. **quom,** causal, "because," takes the indicative in old Latin, the subjunctive in the classical period.

27. **huic** =*mihi*. "Ah, it comes hard on this poor fellow. They've disbanded his regiment of Beefeaters" (Lindsay).

dolet. In old Latin verbs of feeling are used more often impersonally than personally.

28. **quia** =*quod* (colloquial).

30. **imperare exercitum** was the technical phrase at Rome for summoning the Comitia Centuriata (which was originally a military organisation). *Remittere*, "to dismiss," is also technical.

31. **prouinciam**, technically, "a magistrate's sphere of administration"; hence, in general terms, "duty, office."

fugito, frequentative of *fugio*, "to avoid, shun."

32. **quoi** =*cui*, and refers to Philopolemus.

34. **multigeneribus** (*multus-genus*), "of many kinds," a word used only by Plautus.

35 seq. A succession of puns on *pistor* (a miller, the Roman equivalent to a baker) and *Pistoria* (a town in Etruria); *panis* (a loaf) and *Panna* (a town in Samnium); *placenta* (a cake) and *Placentia* (a town in Gallia Cispadana); *turdus* (a thrush) and *Turdetani* (a people of Southern Spain); *ficedula* (a small bird which was considered a great delicacy at table) and *Ficedulae* (a town the situation of which is unknown). Perhaps "Scone, Sandwich, Eigg, Beer and Rum."

39. **opus sunt**. This construction occurs in all periods of Latin, but in a negative sentence, and in an interrogative sentence after *quid*, *opus est* with the ablative is almost always found.

41. **hic qualis...**, literally, "what a general is this man now a civilian," i.e. "what a military genius lies under this civilian's cloak" (Lindsay).

43. **in his diebus**, "in a few days."

48. **nusquam** (*ne-usquam*) means "nowhere," "not in any place," but sometimes (as here) "not to any place." A similar confusion is seen with the word *intus*, which properly means "within," but sometimes has the sense of "from within," e.g. *Most.* 675 *euoca aliquem intus ad te*. Thus in English we say "Where are you going?" instead of "Whither are you going?"

quod sciam, "as far as I know"; the subjunctive is used in phrases that restrict a general statement.

49. **natalis dies**, "birthday."

50. **propterea** (*propter-ea*), "on that account," often used *à propos* of something just said.

51. **facete dictum**, "splendid idea!"

pauxillum =*pauxillo*; trans., "with very poor fare."

52. **ne...modo** =*dummodo...ne*. Ergasilus feels that a line must be drawn somewhere.

53. **adsiduo**, an adverb, =*semper*.

54. **roga emptum**, "come, name your price"; a technical formula in transactions of sale.

meliorem, sc. *condicionem* ("offer") from the line below. This too has the sound of a legal formula.

56. **addicam** ="knock down, strike off." Ergasilus "strikes himself off," i.e. promises himself to Hegio as a guest, provided that he does not in the meantime get a better invitation.

legibus, "conditions."

57. **profundum** (=*uenter*) and **fundum** (farm); a pun. Perhaps "acher" and "acre" (Lindsay): or "empty state" and "estate."

58. **temperi**, see note on "The Miser," sc. ii, l. 51.

59. **lepus**, "a hare," **ictis**, "a weasel." Perhaps a more natural English rendering would be, "you've got your sprat, now go and fish for your whale."

60. **commetat**, frequentative of *commeo*, "to go." "My bill of fare goes the stony way."

61. I.e. "not more than *my* bill of fare."

62. **calceatis dentibus**, "with teeth booted and spurred." Note the metaphor.

63. **essitas**, frequentative of *edo*.

64. **terrestris**, "of the earth." "The pig is a beast of the earth," i.e. "such a diet does not preclude the possibility of pork."

65. **multis holeribus**, "I mean, largely vegetarian."

curato aegrotos domi, literally, "look after sick men at your house," i.e. "open a hospital."

66. **numquid uis**, "Is there anything more?" A regular form of leave-taking.

67. **ratiunculam**, diminutive, "little account." *Rationem subducere* =to balance an account by subtracting one set of items from another.

68. **tarpezita** =*trapezita* (Greek τραπεζίτης, from τράπεζα, a money-changer's table), "a banker." For this change in the position of *r* cf. *accerso* for *arcesso* ("The Twins," sc. i, l. 22).

69. **ire dixeram** =*me iturum esse dixeram*. This construction occurs elsewhere in Plautus, e.g. *Most.* 621 *egon dicam dare?* "Am I to say I will grant it?" and "The Miser," sc. i, l. 64.

dixeram for *dixi*. Cf. "A Strange Dilemma," sc. i, l. 48.

iuero for *ibo*. This use of the future perfect for the future is common in colloquial Latin.

VIII

A Business Transaction

Scene I

1. **beas,** "that's all right" (ironically, in reply to *taceo*); literally, "you gladden [me]." The adjective *beatus* is really the past participle of this somewhat rare verb, *beo*. Cp. "The Parasite," l. 12.

2. **Pellaeo,** "belonging to Pella," an ancient city of Macedonia. The Greeks never regarded the Macedonians as true Greeks, hence a merchant from Macedonia would be looked upon by these two Greek slaves as an easy prey to their trickery. Arcadian asses were famous in Greece.

3. **atriensem,** the steward, or chief servant of the household. The word is derived from *atrium*, the forecourt of the house, which was the common meeting-place of the family. *Atrium* is in its turn derived from *ater*, black, because the walls were blackened by the smoke from the hearth. The *atriensis* in this case is Saurea, mentioned in the next line.

8. **uetulos,** diminutive adjective from *uetus*, "somewhat old," the "somewhat" being here sarcastic.

femina, a rare plural form of the neuter noun *femur*, a thigh (usual form *femora*). "With their hoofs worn away up to their hocks."

9. **subuectabant** contains two ideas, that of holding up (*sub*) and carrying (*uecto*, frequentative of *ueho*).

10. **memor es probe,** "you have a fine memory."

11. **tostrina.** The barber's shop was a common resort and centre of gossip in antiquity.

12. **Demaenetum,** an old man, master of Leonida and Libanus.

17. **uero,** simply an adversative particle.

18. **quoniam** =*quum iam*: always purely temporal in Plautus.

19. **facetum,** "fine."

20. **med** =*me*.

21. This line shows clearly the common distinction in use between *nosco* and *scio*.

24. **praesto,** "at hand, ready."

26. **consili,** partitive genitive after *quid*.

dice, old form for *dic*.

27. **interuortam,** intercept.

aduentor =*aduena*, i.e. the *mercator*.

28. **exasceato,** hewn out; from *ascia* (Greek ἀξίνη) an axe.
30. Note the alliteration in this line.
sorsum =*seorsum*, "aside" (abbreviated from *se-vorsum*).
31. **ulmeos,** "made of elm-trees, like elms," from being thrashed with cudgels of elm. Tr., "birched."
32. **Argyrippus,** the son of Demaenetus, in urgent need of the money.
34. **defrudare** =*defraudare*, to cheat.
operam promiscam dare, "give help in either case," "stand by us whichever it was."
35. **ut,** how; **sumus,** early use of the indicative in indirect questions.
39. **quid ais?** translate, "I say." Note **mălam.**
42. **malo cum auspicio,** a Roman touch, cp. "The Miser," sc. ii, l. 44. "You will find you have chosen an unlucky day for changing your name."
43. **patitor,** future imperative (deponent), for *patere*.
45. **ne nega,** common Plautine construction; cp. sc. iii, l. 56. **hostire,** "to retaliate."
48. **quin** =*quī* (old ablative) +*ne*, "why not," used only in exhortations, not in asking for information. *Quin facis* = "why do you not do?" equivalent to the imperative "do."
officium, "part," i.e. (1) your part in this scheme, and (2) your usual part of running away.

SCENE II

2. **puere,** old vocative of *puer*; the original nominative was *pueros*.
4. **si quid audis,** "if you're not deaf."
5. **sanun** =*sanus-ne*.
6. **conseruas.** Libanus refers to the doors as his "fellow-slaves," in order to show to what an extent he identifies himself with his master's household.
8. **periclum est** is followed by the same construction as verbs of fearing.
10. **mŏrata** (from *mōs*), to be distinguished from *mŏrata* (e.g. sc. iii, l. 7) (from *mora*). "The door has been trained in this way."
11. **calcitro,** rare noun, derived from *calco,* to kick.
14. **mage,** shortened form of *magis,* found chiefly in poetry.
17. **qui pro istuc?** "what for?" Anastrophe of the preposition.
20. **rufulus,** diminutive; "rather red." Red hair was the

conventional mark of the stage-slave. Old men wore white hair, and young men black.

23. **ipsum adeo**; *adeo* is often used after pronouns, like the Greek γε, to give a further shade of emphasis. Cp. αὐτός γε.

contuor =*contueor*.

24. **quisque** =*quicunque*.

25. **Aeacidinus**, adjective, "characteristic of a descendant of Aeacus," i.e. of Achilles, Aeacus' grandson.

Scene III

1. **negoti**, partitive genitive after *quid*.

magni, genitive of price.

2. **nullus**, used adverbially for *non*.

3. **ne**, see note on "The Twins," sc. ii, l. 11.

5. **libertum**, sarcastic. "Is Libanus a freedman," says Leonida, "that I should give him greeting?" (Then turning to Libanus) "Have you been set free?"

9. **precator**, predicative; translate, "to plead for you."

11. **Saurea**. The merchant here addresses Leonida, under the impression that he is Saurea, the *atriensis*.

14. **perdere**, the causative verb of *pereo*, "to make him perish," "to be his undoing."

15. **semel**, emphatic, and contrasted with *centiens* in the next line.

16. **ogganniam**, "snarl, growl"; found only in early Latin.

20. **bullas**, here "door-knobs": often used of gold amulets worn by boys of free birth.

21. "I have to walk about after you with a stick, just as if I were lame."

24. **hara**, a pig-sty; from the same root as *co-hors* (Greek χορός), something enclosed, i.e. a poultry-yard.

25. **em ergo hoc tibi**. With these words Leonida gives Libanus a blow. "There now, take that."

26. **uectura**. "Has anyone paid the carriage on the olive-oil?"

27. **uicario**, "your deputy," a subtle compliment, as a slave would not normally hold so exalted a position as to have a deputy. Leonida angrily discounts the compliment in the next line.

29. **eo**, comparative ablative dependent on *pluris*.

30. **Exaerambo**, a name otherwise unknown.

33. **sic dedero**. "That's what I like. When I trusted him

before, I was hardly able to extract the money from him a
year after."

34. **scribit nummos,** "he is writing his cheque."

35. **mercedem.** Dromo was a slave hired out, whose wages
went to his master.

37. Construe *ut [id] operis ecficeret quod sibi sit locatum.*

38. **utendos dedi,** "lent."

40. **odio,** here = "insolence."

iam satis tu, sc. *locutus es.*

42. **adeam,** deliberative subjunctive depending on *optumum
est.*

49. **Demaeneto ero praesente,** to be taken together as an
ablative absolute.

tibi, dative with *reddam.*

51. **rem saluam exhibebo,** "I will guarantee that it shall be
all right."

54. **magni,** genitive of price. "I don't care."

duit, old subjunctive of *do.* "He need not give it if he does
not want to."

58. See note on "A Strange Dilemma, sc. i, l. 57. *Sane* is
frequently thus used with the imperative.

60. **incerto,** adjective agreeing with *nemini homini,* meaning
"unreliable, whom I can't depend on."

61. **caue,** addressed to Libanus.

62. **ferox,** i.e. the merchant. "He is proud at having
the handling of...."

63. **aufer te,** "get away home," addressed to the merchant.

65. Leonida incites Libanus to urge the merchant again.

66. **nihili,** "it's of no importance" (genitive of price).

perge; Leonida prompts Libanus to further efforts.

68. **crura,** the legs of Libanus.

74. **in ius uoco te,** "I summon you to (the praetor's) court,"
the ordinary legal phrase: but of course legally a slave could
not be thus summoned.

75. "By heaven, I will get satisfaction at the expense of
your back."

uae te. The usual phrase is *uae tibi. Te* here is accusative.

77. **maledicis,** from *maledicus,* adjective.

84. **praefiscini,** "without offence"; from *fascinum,* the evil
eye.

88. **lupus est homo homini.** The wolf, a common animal
in ancient Italy, appears frequently in Roman proverbs.
Another is *hac urget lupus, hac canis angit,* i.e. "between two
fires" (Horace).

89. **capitulo**, diminutive of *caput*, in the sense of "a person." *Hoc caput* = I.

91. **frugi**, indeclinable adjective, meaning "honest."

peculium, a slave's own money. His money could not be counted because he had none. He intends the *mercator* to understand that it could not be counted because he has so much.

95. **percontatus me ex aliis**, "if you enquired about me from other people."

96. **hau negassim**, sarcastic, "Oh, very likely."

IX

The Carthaginian

Prologus. Most of the extant prologues to Plautus' plays were composed by writers now unknown, after Plautus' lifetime. They were recited, as will be seen at the end of this extract, by an actor who was afterwards to take a part in the drama itself. Sometimes this actor appears simply as "Prologus" (as in the *Poenulus*, *Asinaria* and *Captiui*), sometimes as one of the characters in the play (as Mercury in the *Amphitruo*), and sometimes as an abstract character, in some way appropriate to the story (as the *Lars Familiaris* in the *Aulularia*). Some plays (e.g. *Miles Gloriosus*) are without prologues.

1. **Καρχηδόνιος.** We do not know the name of the author of the Greek original. Several of Plautus' prologues tell the original from which he had translated in each case. Thus from the prologue to the *Rudens* we learn that the Greek author was Diphilus. (From other sources we know that the play was the πήρα.) In the prologue to the *Asinaria* we are told that the original was the ὀναγός of Demophilus.

2. **Pultiphagonides**, contemptuous: "Pottage-eater's-son." But both Romans and Greeks ate *puls* as much as did the Carthaginians.

3. **rationes**, here a pun, meaning (1) reckoning, assessment, (2) matter or business; the first meaning leads to the introduction of *censeo*, "to assess," and *iuratores*, "assessment clerks." Translate: "You've got the name: now hear the rest of the account. The account to be reckoned up here is the plot. The proper place for a plot is the particular stage it

is set on. You are the clerks who have to reckon the account."

7. **patruelis**, adjective, "belonging to a father's brother." *Fratres patrueles* are cousins on the father's side. Contrast *fratres consobrini*, cousins on the mother's side.

8. **ditiis**, contracted form of *diuitiis*.

9. **emortuos**, old and rare form of *mortuos* (*mortuus*): translate, "quite dead."

10. **propterea**, "for this reason," points forward to *quia*.

12. **filius**, Agorastocles.

13. **ab**, "on account of, in consequence of," giving a motive.

14. **surrupitur** = *surripitur*.

19. **uiatico** (fr. *uia*), journey-money. It was customary among the Greeks to bury an obol with each dead person, in order that he might be able to pay his fare to Charon, who would ferry him across the Styx. The reference here is simply to show how completely the dead man had willed away his property to his cousin.

20. **Calydonem**, a town in Aetolia.

23. **hospitalem filium**, "as a son by virtue of hospitality." **imprudens**, "unsuspecting, little guessing the future."

27. **reuortor**, metaphorical. **rusus** = *rursus*.

31. **senex**, *Hanno*, the Carthaginian.

33. **quadrimula**, rare diminutive of *quadrima* (which is derived from *quattuor* and the same root as *hiems*); "a little thing of four years old."

34. **Magaribus**, ablative plural of *Magara* (Megara), for *Magaris*.

35. **Anactorium**, in Acarnania, on the west coast of Greece.

40. **quaesti**, business, trade. For the form see note on "The Miser," sc. i, l. 39.

41. **ecflictim**, "desperately": adverb formed from *ecfligo*, to strike dead. For the ending *-im* cf. *assulatim*, "The Twins," sc. i, l. 6.

perit, transitive, "pines away with love for."

48. **quoiatis** = *cuiatis*, genitive of *cuias*, interrogative pronoun, meaning "of what country?" Here, "the daughter of a man of what nationality?" Translate, "of what nationality her father was." For the ending *-as* cp. *nostras*, "of our country."

52. **Poenus plane est**, a commentary on *dissimulat sciens se scire* (notice the juxtaposition of *sciens* and *scire*). Carthaginian *fides* was notorious.

54. **harunc** = *harum.*

55. **tenetis**, a pun on "understand," and "hold." Translate, "Have you got that? Well then, if you've got it, take it along. Mind you don't hurt yourselves, do: and now have done with it." This joke is supposed to be received with roars of laughter, and after the interruption thus caused, the Prologue resumes, "*paene oblitus....*"

62. **ibo**, i.e. I must now go in and change to another character.

63. **quod restat**, "as for the remainder of the story, others remain to explain it to you."

APPENDIX

METRE

One of the most common metres, and perhaps the simplest, used by Plautus, is the iambic trimeter. It consists of six feet, of which the basis is the iamb: but dactyls, spondees, tribrachs and anapaests are admitted as variants to all feet except the sixth.

An example in this book is scene i from the *Aulularia*:

exi in|quam age ex|i : exeun|dum hercle ti|bi hinc est |

                                      foras

circum|specta|trix cum ocu|lis e|missi|ciis.

nam qur | me mise|ram uer|beras? | ut mise|ra sis,

atque ut | te dig|nam mala | malam ae|tatem ex|igas

Other extracts in this metre are those from: *Mostellaria; Miles Gloriosus; Rudens* (sc. i); *Menaechmi* (sc. i, 20–end; sc. ii, 1–10); *Captiui; Poenulus.*

Very common, but more intricate, are the trochaic septenarii. A line in this metre consists of seven feet and a half, and the basis is the trochee. It allows of many variations—tribrachs, spondees, dactyls and anapaests—in the first six feet. The seventh is always a trochee or a tribrach.

An example in this book is the first extract from the *Amphitruo*, e.g.:

non ede|pol nunc | ubi ter|rarum | sim sci|o si | quis ro|get

neque mi|ser me | commo|uere | possum | prae for|midi|ne.

ili|cet : man|data e|ri pe|rierunt | una et | Sosi|a.

uerum | certumst | confi|denter | hominem | contra |

                                        conlo|qui.

Other extracts in this metre are from: *Amphitruo* (sc. ii, 43–end); *Menaechmi* (sc. i, 1–18; sc. ii, 11–end); *Aulularia* (sc. ii, 44–end); *Asinaria* (sc. i).

Other metres.

Amphitruo, scene ii, 1–23—**bacchiac**.

age i tu | secundum : | sequor sup|sequor te.

scelestis|sumum te ar|bitror. nam | quamobrem?

Rudens, scene ii, is intricate from the point of view of scansion. Lines 1–15 are mainly bacchiac, e.g. l. 9:

sed id si | parate | curaui ut | cauerem.

Lines 16–34 are mainly cretic, e.g. l. 19:

quae mihi | si foret | salua sal|tem labor.

Scene iii, lines 1–8, is **anapaestic** (8 feet in a line), e.g. l. 1:

quid mihi | meliust | quid magis | in remst | quam a

cor|pore ui|tam ut se|cludam?

The rest of the extract is deliberately composed in a variety of metres (chiefly bacchiac and cretic), in order to express the emotional atmosphere of the situation.

Aulularia, scene ii, lines 1–6, are trochaic, l. 1:

atta|tae ci|ues popu|lares|inco|lae acco|lae adue|nae omnes.

Lines 12–42 are **versus Reiziani**, consisting of an iambic dimeter followed by an acephalous glyconic.

redi. quo | fugis|nunc? tene | tene. ‖ Quid stolide clamas?

quia ad tres | uiros | iam ego de|feram ‖ nomen tuom.

Quam ob rem?

quia cul|trum habes. | Cocum decet. ‖ Quid comminatu's?

Asinaria, scenes ii and iii, are iambic **septenarii**, each line consisting of seven feet and a half, l. 8:

pol hau | peri|clum est car|dines | ne fori|bus ec|fringan|tur.

Printed in the United States
By Bookmasters